Java Exercises with Data Structures and Algorithms

ISBN: 9798325955266

Copyright © 2024 by Haris Tsetsekas

Table of Contents

1. University Courses 5
2. Restaurant Reservations 9
3. Library 13
4. Contact List 21
5. Priority Todo List 25
6. Songs List 31
7. Task allocation 35
8. Word Frequencies 39
9. Syntax Checker 41
10. Maze Solver 45
11. File Indexer 51
12. Inventory with AVL Tree 57
13. Social Network 63
14. Flights 69
15. MNIST Image Comparison 75
16. HTTP Server with Caching 81
17. Distributed Auction 87

1. University Courses

Let's create a program that will handle the enrollment for university courses. Each course has one or more prerequisites, i.e. courses that must have been completed by a student in order to be able to enroll in the specific one.

Proposed Solution

First of all, we will define the class for a student in the university:

```java
package UniversityCourses;

public class Student {
  public int id;
  public String name;
  public int[] courses;
  public int courseCount;

  public Student(int id, String name, int courseCount, int[] courses) {
    this.id = id;
    this.name = name;
    this.courseCount = courseCount;
    this.courses = courses;
  }
}
```
Listing 1-1: Student.java

This class contains information about the student and the courses that have been completed successfully. The `Courses` array contains the ID of the course.

Next, we define a class for the university courses:

```java
package UniversityCourses;

public class Course {
  public int id;
  public String name;
  public int prereqCount;
  public int[] prereqIDs;

  public Course(int id, String name, int prereqCount, int[] prereqIDs) {
    this.id = id;
    this.name = name;
    this.prereqCount = prereqCount;
    this.prereqIDs = prereqIDs;
  }

  public boolean canEnroll(Student student) {
    for (int prereqId : this.prereqIDs) {
      boolean hasPrereq = false;
      for (int courseId : student.courses) {
        if (courseId == prereqId) {
          hasPrereq = true;
          break;
```

```
            }
        }
        if (!hasPrereq) {
            return false;
        }
    }
    return true;
  }
}
```

Listing 1-2: Course.java

Each course contains an array of the IDs of the prerequisite courses. The class also includes a method that finds out whether a student can enroll at a course. For each prerequisite course, this method tries to match it with a course already taken by the student.

Finally, the main() method:

```
package UniversityCourses;

public class UniversityCourses {
  public static void main(String[] args) {
    Course[] courses = {
        new Course(0, "Intro to Programming", 0, new int[] { -1 }),
        new Course(1, "Data Structures", 1, new int[] { 0 }),
        new Course(2, "Algorithms", 1, new int[] { 1 }),
        new Course(3, "Database Management", 1, new int[] { 0 }),
        new Course(4, "Web Development", 1, new int[] { 0 }),
        new Course(5, "Operating Systems", 2, new int[] { 1, 2 }),
        new Course(6, "Computer Networks", 2, new int[] { 1, 5 }),
        new Course(7, "Software Engineering", 2, new int[] { 1, 2 }),
        new Course(8, "Machine Learning", 2, new int[] { 1, 2 }),
        new Course(9, "Distributed Systems", 1, new int[] { 5 }),
        new Course(10, "Cybersecurity", 2, new int[] { 2, 3 }),
        new Course(11, "Cloud Computing", 2, new int[] { 2, 3 }),
        new Course(12, "Mobile App Development", 1, new int[] { 4 }),
        new Course(13, "Game Development", 1, new int[] { 0 }),
        new Course(14, "Artificial Intelligence", 2, new int[] { 2, 8 }),
        new Course(15, "Big Data Analytics", 2, new int[] { 2, 3 }),
        new Course(16, "Blockchain Technology", 2, new int[] { 2, 3 }),
        new Course(17, "UI/UX Design", 1, new int[] { 14 }),
        new Course(18, "Embedded Systems", 2, new int[] { 1, 5 }),
        new Course(19, "Computer Graphics", 1, new int[] { 0 })
    };

    Student student = new Student(1, "John Doe", 5, new int[] { 0, 1, 2, 3, 4 });

    Course[] targetCourses = {
        courses[13], // Game Development
        courses[16], // Blockchain Technology
        courses[17], // UI/UX Design (student cannot enroll)
        courses[18]  // Embedded Systems
    };
```

```
      System.out.println("Enrollment status for " + student.name + ": ");
      for (int i = 0; i < 4; ++i) {
        if (targetCourses[i].canEnroll(student)) {
          System.out.println("- Can enroll in " + targetCourses[i].name);
        } else {
          System.out.println("- Cannot enroll in " + targetCourses[i].name
            + " due to missing prerequisites.");
        }
      }
    }
  }
}
```

Listing 1-3: UniversityCourses.java

We create sample courses and a sample user that is still at the earlier stages of studies. We then try to find out if this student can enroll at 4 specific courses. We will see that the student will not be able to enroll at the most advanced ones, for lack of successfully completed prerequisite courses.

You can find this project in GitHub:

https://github.com/htset/java_exercises_dsa/tree/master/UniversityCourses

2. Restaurant Reservations

For this exercise, we will create a small program that will create table reservations for a restaurant. Each table is characterized by its capacity. For simplicity, we will split the reservation time in one-hour slots; a reservation can span multiple consecutive slots.

Proposed Solution

First of all, we will define the class for a customer:

```java
package Restaurant;

public class Customer {
  public String name;

  public Customer(String name) {
    this.name = name;
  }
}
```

Listing 2-1: Customer.java

This class contains the name of the customer. It could also include the customer phone number or other details.

Next, we define a class for the restaurant tables:

```java
package Restaurant;

public class Table {
  public int id;
  public int capacity;

  public Table(int id, int capacity) {
    this.id = id;
    this.capacity = capacity;
  }
}
```

Listing 2-2: Table.java

Each table object contains its ID as well as information about its capacity (the number of people it can accommodate).

Next, we define the Reservation class:

```java
package Restaurant;

public class Reservation {
  public Customer customer;
  public Table table;
  public int startTimeSlot;
  public int endTimeSlot;
```

```java
    public Reservation(Customer customer, Table table, int startTimeSlot,
        int endTimeSlot) {
      this.customer = customer;
      this.table = table;
      this.startTimeSlot = startTimeSlot;
      this.endTimeSlot = endTimeSlot;
    }
}
```

Listing 2-3: Reservation.java

Each reservation contains references to `Customer` and `Table` objects. It also contains the starting and the ending time slot (not inclusive).

We also create a `Restaurant` class that will implement the functionality for the creation of new reservations:

```java
package Restaurant;

import java.util.ArrayList;
import java.util.Comparator;
import java.util.List;
import java.util.stream.Collectors;

public class Restaurant {
  private final List<Table> tables = new ArrayList<>();
  private final List<Reservation> reservations = new ArrayList<>();

  public void addTable(Table table) {
    tables.add(table);
  }

  ...
```

Listing 2-4: Restaurant.java

Method `addTable()` adds the reference of a table into the `tables` list.

In method `isTableAvailable()` we use a stream that we obtain from the `reservations` list. We use the `noneMatch()` method of the stream to determine if there exists a table that is not reserved in the specified timeslot.

```java
public boolean isTableAvailable(Table table, int startTimeSlot, int endTimeSlot) {
  return reservations.stream().noneMatch(reservation ->
    reservation.table.id == table.id &&
      ((startTimeSlot >= reservation.startTimeSlot
        && startTimeSlot < reservation.endTimeSlot) ||
       (endTimeSlot > reservation.startTimeSlot
        && endTimeSlot <= reservation.endTimeSlot) ||
       (startTimeSlot <= reservation.startTimeSlot
        && endTimeSlot >= reservation.endTimeSlot)));
}
```

Listing 2-5: Restaurant.java

Method `findAvailableTables()` searches the stream obtained from the `tables` list, in order to find all the tables that are available inside the specified timeslot.

```java
public List<Table> findAvailableTables(int capacity, int startTimeSlot,
   int endTimeSlot) {
   List<Table> availableTables = tables.stream()
       .filter(table -> table.capacity >= capacity
           && isTableAvailable(table, startTimeSlot, endTimeSlot))
       .collect(Collectors.toList());
   availableTables.sort(Comparator.comparingInt(a -> a.capacity));
   return availableTables;
}
```
Listing 2-6: Restaurant.java

We use `filter()` to get only the free tables whose capacity matches or exceed the person count. The selected tables will be collected into a new list by `collect()` method. This list is returned after being sorted in ascending order, according to the table capacity, as we are trying to fill the smallest tables first.

Next, the `addReservation()` method will create a new reservation on the fly and will insert it into the `reservations` list. That's of course, if a suitable table is found. Note that we get the first table in the sorted list, i.e. the table with the smallest capacity.

```java
public void addReservation(String name, int capacity, int startSlot, int endSlot) {
   List<Table> availableTables = findAvailableTables(capacity, startSlot, endSlot);
   if (!availableTables.isEmpty()) {
      reservations.add(new Reservation(new Customer(name),
          availableTables.get(0), startSlot, endSlot));
      System.out.println("Reservation successfully added.");
   } else {
      System.out.println("No available tables for the requested time slot.");
   }
}
```
Listing 2-7: Restaurant.java

Next, we have a method to print all the reservations in the console:

```java
public void printReservations() {
   System.out.println("All reservations:");
   for (Reservation reservation : reservations) {
      System.out.println("Customer: " + reservation.customer.name +
          ", Table Capacity: " + reservation.table.capacity +
          ", Start Time Slot: " + reservation.startTimeSlot +
          ", End Time Slot: " + reservation.endTimeSlot);
   }
}
```
Listing 2-8: Restaurant.java

Finally, in the `main()` method, we add tables to the `Restaurant` object and try to make reservations for specific capacities and timeslots. Some will be successful, but for others there will not be any table available. At the end, we print all the available reservations in the system.

```java
public static void main(String[] args) {
    Restaurant restaurant = new Restaurant();

    //Add tables
    restaurant.addTable(new Table(1, 6));
    restaurant.addTable(new Table(2, 4));
    restaurant.addTable(new Table(3, 2));

    //Find available tables for a new reservation
    restaurant.addReservation("Customer 1", 4, 1, 3);
    restaurant.addReservation("Customer 2", 6, 2, 4);
    restaurant.addReservation("Customer 3", 4, 3, 5);
    restaurant.addReservation("Customer 4", 4, 1, 3);

    restaurant.printReservations();
  }
}
```

Listing 2-9: Restaurant.java

You can find this project in GitHub:

https://github.com/htset/java_exercises_dsa/tree/master/Restaurant

3. Library

Here we will create a console application for a library. Users will be able to enter books and list all the titles available in the library. They will also be able to lend books, return books as well as list all the book lending events. The books and the lending events will be stored in text files.

Proposed Solution

Let's begin with the definition of the Book and LendingEvent classes:

```
package Library;

public class Book {
  public String title;
  public String author;
  public int available;
}
```
Listing 3-1: Book.java

```
package Library;

import java.time.LocalDateTime;

public class LendingEvent {
  public String bookTitle;
  public String userName;
  public LocalDateTime lendingDate;
  public int returned;
}
```
Listing 3-2: LendingEvent.java

For each book, we record the title and the author. We also keep information about whether it is available or is currently lent (1 or 0 respectively).

For each lending event we record the book title and the name of the library user that has borrowed it. We also keep the lending date as well as an integer value of whether it has been returned or not (1 or 0 respectively).

We also define the Library class, that contains all the functionality for adding and displaying book information:

```
package Library;

import java.io.*;
import java.time.LocalDateTime;
import java.util.Scanner;

public class Library {
  private static final String BooksFilename = "books.txt";
```

```
private static final String LendingFilename = "lending_events.txt";

...
```

Listing 3-3: Library.java

The first method of class `Library` is used to add a new book in library catalog:

```java
public void addBook() throws IOException {
  try (PrintWriter file = new PrintWriter(new FileWriter(BooksFilename, true))) {
    Book book = new Book();
    Scanner scanner = new Scanner(System.in);
    System.out.print("Book title: ");
    book.title = scanner.nextLine();

    System.out.print("Author: ");
    book.author = scanner.nextLine();

    //Mark book as available
    book.available = 1;

    file.println(book.title + "|" + book.author + "|" + book.available);
  }
  System.out.println("Book added successfully.");
}
```

Listing 3-4: Library.java

At the beginning, we open the books file using a `PrintWriter` object. The second parameter to the constructor is *true*, which means that we will append to the end of the file and the current contents will not be erased.

After we get the book title and author from the user, we write the new book object at the end of the file. The following format is used:

```
book title|book author|Available (0 or 1)
```

Next, we implement the listing of the books:

```java
public void listBooks() throws IOException {
  //check if text file exists
  if (!new File(BooksFilename).exists()) {
    System.out.println("No books entered so far");
    return;
  }

  System.out.println("Books available in the library:");
  try (BufferedReader file = new BufferedReader(new FileReader(BooksFilename))) {
    String line;
    while ((line = file.readLine()) != null) {
      String[] parts = line.split("\\|");
      System.out.println("Title: " + parts[0]);
      System.out.println("Author: " + parts[1]);
```

```java
      System.out.println("Available: "
          + (parts[2].equals("1") ? "True" : "False"));
      System.out.println("--------------------------------");
    }
  }
}
```

Listing 3-5: Library.java

Here, we open the file from the beginning and we use `readLine()` to read the details of each book from the text file.

We proceed with the book lending functionality:

```java
public void lendBook() throws IOException {
  //check if text file exists
  if (!new File(BooksFilename).exists()) {
    System.out.println("No books entered so far");
    return;
  }

  String bookTitle, userName;
  Scanner scanner = new Scanner(System.in);
  System.out.print("Enter the title of the book to lend: ");
  bookTitle = scanner.nextLine();

  //Get a string array of all lines in file
  String[] lines = new BufferedReader(new FileReader(BooksFilename))
      .lines().toArray(String[]::new);
  boolean bookFound = false;

  for (int i = 0; i < lines.length; i++) {
    //Split line into book details
    String[] parts = lines[i].split("\\|");
    if (parts[0].equals(bookTitle) && parts[2].equals("1")) {
      lines[i] = parts[0] + "|" + parts[1] + "|0";
      bookFound = true;

      System.out.print("Enter your name: ");
      userName = scanner.nextLine();

      //Write lending event into file
      try (PrintWriter lendingFile
              = new PrintWriter(new FileWriter(LendingFilename, true))) {
        lendingFile.println(bookTitle + "|" + userName + "|"
            + LocalDateTime.now() + "|0");
      }

      System.out.println("Book '" + bookTitle + "' has been lent to "
          + userName + ".");
      break;
    }
  }
```

```java
    if (!bookFound) {
      System.out.println("Book '" + bookTitle + "' not found or not available.");
    }

    //Write books back to file (overwrite file)
    try (PrintWriter file = new PrintWriter(new FileWriter(BooksFilename))) {
      for (String line : lines) {
        file.println(line);
      }
    }
  }
```

Listing 3-6: Library.java

We first try to find the requested book by reading all the entries from the books file with `.lines().toArray(String[]::new)`. The book entries will be stored in an array of strings. `String[]::new` is a function that makes new `String` arrays. It will be called by `toArray()` in order to create the new array.

We iterate this array and we split each entry into the book details (title, author, availability). When we find the book (and if it is available), we mark it as not currently available.

Afterwards, we record the lending event by writing a new entry at the end of the respective binary file. Finally, we write all the entries in the array back to the books text file, overwriting the file.

Next, we present the functionality for returning a book:

```java
public void returnBook() throws IOException {
  if (!new File(LendingFilename).exists()) {
    System.out.println("No lending events entered so far");
    return;
  }

  String bookTitle;
  Scanner scanner = new Scanner(System.in);
  System.out.print("Enter the title of the book to return: ");
  bookTitle = scanner.nextLine();

  //Get a string array of all lines in file
  String[] booksLines = new BufferedReader(new FileReader(BooksFilename))
      .lines().toArray(String[]::new);
  boolean bookFound = false;

  for (int i = 0; i < booksLines.length; i++) {
    String[] parts = booksLines[i].split("\\|");
    if (parts[0].equals(bookTitle) && parts[2].equals("0")) {
      booksLines[i] = parts[0] + "|" + parts[1] + "|1";
      bookFound = true;

      //Get all lending events
```

```java
      String[] lendingLines = new BufferedReader(new FileReader(LendingFilename))
          .lines().toArray(String[]::new);

      for (int j = 0; j < lendingLines.length; j++) {
        parts = lendingLines[j].split("\\|");
        if (parts[0].equals(bookTitle) && parts[3].equals("0")) {
          lendingLines[j] = parts[0] + "|" + parts[1] + "|" + parts[2] + "|1";
          System.out.println("Book '" + bookTitle + "' has been returned.");
          break;
        }
      }

      //Write lending events back to file
      try (PrintWriter lendingFile
            = new PrintWriter(new FileWriter(LendingFilename))) {
        for (String line : lendingLines) {
          lendingFile.println(line);
        }
      }
      break;
    }
  }

  if (!bookFound) {
    System.out.println("Book '" + bookTitle + "' not found or already returned.");
  }

  //Write books back to file
  try (PrintWriter file = new PrintWriter(new FileWriter(BooksFilename))) {
    for (String line : booksLines) {
      file.println(line);
    }
  }
}
```

Listing 3-7: Library.java

Here, we read again all the book file entries into an array of strings, and we try to find the requested file. Then, we read all the book lending events from the respective file and we search for the lending event of the specific book.

If we find the event, then we change its status to "returned" and we write all the entries back to the lending file. Finally, we also store all the book entries into the respective file, after having changed the book availability status back to 1 again.

Now, let's see the events listing method:

```java
public void listLendingEvents() throws IOException {
  if (!new File(LendingFilename).exists()) {
    System.out.println("No lending events entered so far");
    return;
  }
```

```java
      System.out.println("Lending events:");
      try (BufferedReader file = new BufferedReader(new FileReader(LendingFilename))) {
        String line;
        while ((line = file.readLine()) != null) {
          String[] parts = line.split("\\|");
          System.out.println("Book Title: " + parts[0]);
          System.out.println("User Name: " + parts[1]);
          System.out.println("Lending Date: " + parts[2]);
          System.out.println("Returned: " + (parts[3].equals("1") ? "True" : "False"));
          System.out.println("------------------------------");
        }
      }
    }
  }
```
Listing 3-8: Library.java

And finally, the `main()` method that handles the interaction with the user:

```java
  public static void main(String[] args) throws IOException {
    Library lib = new Library();
    int choice;
    Scanner scanner = new Scanner(System.in);
    do {
      System.out.println("\n1. Add a book\n2. List all books\n" +
          "3. Lend a book\n4. Return a book\n5. List lending events\n0. Exit");
      System.out.print("Enter your choice: ");
      choice = scanner.nextInt();

      switch (choice) {
        case 1:
          lib.addBook();
          break;
        case 2:
          lib.listBooks();
          break;
        case 3:
          lib.lendBook();
          break;
        case 4:
          lib.returnBook();
          break;
        case 5:
          lib.listLendingEvents();
          break;
        case 0:
          System.out.println("Exiting.");
          break;
        default:
          System.out.println("Invalid choice. Please try again.");
          break;
      }

    } while (choice != 0);
  }
}
```
Listing 3-9: Library.java

You can find this project in GitHub:

https://github.com/htset/java_exercises_dsa/tree/master/Library

4. Contact List

In this exercise, we will create a list that will store the names and the phone numbers of our contacts. For faster search performance, the contacts will be stored in a *hash map* structure.

Proposed Solution

A *hash map*, also known as a *hash table*, is a data structure that efficiently organizes and retrieves data based on key-value pairs. It employs a technique called *hashing*, where each key is mapped to a unique index in an array using a hash function. This mapping allows for rapid insertion, deletion, and retrieval of values based on their associated keys.

In cases where multiple keys hash to the same index (known as *collisions*), hash maps often employ strategies such as *chaining* to handle these collisions gracefully and maintain performance.

Here is the definition of the classes used:

```java
class Contact {
  public String name;
  public String phone;
  public Contact next;

  public Contact() {
    this.name = null;
    this.phone = null;
    this.next = null;
  }
}

public class ContactList {
  private static final int HASH_SIZE = 100;
  private Contact[] bucketTable;

  ...
```

Listing 4-1: ContactList.java

The `ContactList` class contains a table of 100 entries. Each entry contains a reference to a `Contact` object. The `Contact` class contains the name and the phone number, as well as a reference to another `Contact` object, making it a linked list node. Essentially, the `ContactList` class is an array of linked lists; in this way the contact list can expand as we add new elements, avoiding collisions.

A contact will be inserted into one of the buckets according to its specific hash number. We will use a hash function that will create a number between 0 and 99 based on the contact's name string:

```java
  private int hash(String name) {
    int hash = 5381;
    for (int i = 0; i < name.length(); i++) {
```

```
    hash = ((hash << 5) + hash) + name.charAt(i);
  }
  return Math.abs(hash) % HASH_SIZE;
}
```

Listing 4-2: ContactList.java

This method is based on a hash function written by Daniel J. Bernstein (also know as *djb*)[1]. This method returns the index of the hash map, where we should insert the specific contact.

In the class constructor we initialize the buckets with nulls:

```
public ContactList() {
  bucketTable = new Contact[HASH_SIZE];
  for (int i = 0; i < HASH_SIZE; i++) {
    bucketTable[i] = null;
  }
}
```

Listing 4-3: ContactList.java

Here is the code for the contact addition:

```
public void contactAdd(String name, String phone) {
  //get index from contact name
  int hashIndex = hash(name);
  Contact newContact = new Contact();
  newContact.name = name;
  newContact.phone = phone;
  newContact.next = bucketTable[hashIndex];
  bucketTable[hashIndex] = newContact;
}
```

Listing 4-4: ContactList.java

We first calculate the hash index based on the contact's name and then we create a new Contact object. After populating the object properties, we insert the object at the beginning of the respective bucket.

Here is the code for contact removal:

```
public void contactRemove(String name) {
  int index = hash(name);
  Contact contact = bucketTable[index];
  Contact previous = null;

  while (contact != null) {
    if (contact.name.equals(name)) {
      if (previous == null) {
        //Contact to remove is the head of the list
        bucketTable[index] = contact.next;
```

---

[1] http://www.cse.yorku.ca/~oz/hash.html

```
      } else {
        //Contact to remove is not the head of the list
        previous.next = contact.next;
      }
      System.out.println("Contact '" + name + "' removed successfully.");
      return;
    }
    previous = contact;
    contact = contact.next;
  }
  System.out.println("Contact '" + name + "' not found.");
}
```

Listing 4-5: ContactList.java

To remove an entry, we first need to get its hash value. We use this integer value as the index to get the respective bucket. We then search the bucket entries, one by one, until we locate the specific contact. We then remove the entry from the buckets, in the same way we remove a node from a linked list.

Next, the code for contact search is presented:

```java
public void contactSearch(String name) {
  int hashIndex = hash(name);
  Contact contact = bucketTable[hashIndex];
  while (contact != null) {
    if (contact.name.equals(name)) {
      System.out.println("Name: " + contact.name
          + "\nPhone Number: " + contact.phone);
      return;
    }
    contact = contact.next;
  }
  System.out.println("Contact '" + name + "' not found.");
}
```

Listing 4-6: ContactList.java

Finally, in the `main()` method, we create a phonebook and we use it to add, remove and search contacts:

```java
public static void main(String[] args) {
  ContactList phonebook = new ContactList();
  phonebook.contactAdd("John", "235454545");
  phonebook.contactAdd("Jane", "775755454");
  phonebook.contactAdd("George", "4344343477");

  phonebook.contactSearch("John");
  phonebook.contactSearch("Alex");
  phonebook.contactSearch("George");

  phonebook.contactRemove("Jake");
  phonebook.contactRemove("Jane");
  phonebook.contactSearch("Jane");
```

```
    }
}
```
Listing 4-7: ContactList.java

You can find this project in GitHub:

https://github.com/htset/java_exercises_dsa/tree/master/ContactList

5. Priority Todo List

We are going to implement a simple todo list application. Each entry will contain the task description as well as a number that will signify its priority (top priority is equal to 1).

The todo list will be implemented using a *linked list*. Apart from the options to add, delete and display tasks, there will also be functionality to sort the linked list using *bubble sort*.

Proposed Solution

First let's see the `main()` method, in *Todo.java*:

```java
package Todo;
import java.util.Scanner;

public class Todo {
  public static void main(String[] args) {
    TodoList list = new TodoList();
    Scanner scanner = new Scanner(System.in);

    int choice = 0;
    String description;
    int priority;
    int index;

    do {
      try {
        System.out.println("\nTo-Do List Manager");
        System.out.println("1. Add Task");
        System.out.println("2. Remove Task");
        System.out.println("3. Display Tasks");
        System.out.println("4. Sort Tasks by Priority");
        System.out.println("0. Exit");
        System.out.print("Enter your choice: ");
        choice = Integer.parseInt(scanner.nextLine());

        switch (choice) {
          case 1:
            System.out.print("Enter task description: ");
            description = scanner.nextLine();
            System.out.print("Enter priority: ");
            priority = Integer.parseInt(scanner.nextLine());
            list.addTask(description, priority);
            System.out.println("Task added successfully.");
            break;
          case 2:
            System.out.print("Enter number of task to remove: ");
            index = Integer.parseInt(scanner.nextLine());
            list.removeTask(index - 1);
            System.out.println("Task removed successfully.");
            break;
          case 3:
            System.out.println("List of tasks:");
            list.displayTasks();
```

```
          break;
        case 4:
          list.sortTasks();
          System.out.println("Tasks sorted by priority.");
          break;
        case 0:
          System.out.println("Exiting...");
          break;
        default:
          System.out.println("Invalid choice. Please try again.");
          break;
      }
    } catch (NumberFormatException e) {
      System.out.println("Invalid input. Please enter a number.");
    }
  } while (choice != 0);
  scanner.close();
  }
}
```

Listing 5-1: Todo.java

The main method handles the user input and calls the respective methods of the todo list.

Here is the definition of the Task class that makes the objects of the linked list structure:

```
package Todo;

public class Task {
  public String description;
  public int priority;
  public Task next;

  public Task() {
    this.description = null;
    this.priority = 0;
    this.next = null;
  }
}
```

Listing 5-2: Task.java

The linked list consists of Task nodes that get linked one to the other via the next reference. The head variable points to the first element in the list:

```
package Todo;

public class TodoList {
  private Task head;
  private int size;

  public TodoList() {
    head = null;
    size = 0;
```

}
...

Listing 5-3: TodoList.java

The class constructor initializes the linked list structure.

The `addTask()` method creates a new task node and inserts it at the end of the linked list:

```java
public void addTask(String description, int priority) {
  Task task = new Task();
  task.description = description;
  task.priority = priority;
  task.next = null;

  if (head == null) {
    //List is empty
    head = task;
  } else {
    Task temp = head;
    //Find the last node
    while (temp.next != null) {
      temp = temp.next;
    }
    //Insert the new task after the last node
    temp.next = task;
  }
  size++;
}
```

Listing 5-4: TodoList.java

Next, we define the `removeTask()` method:

```java
public void removeTask(int index) {
  if (head == null) {
    System.out.println("List is empty.");
    return;
  }

  if (index == 0) {
    //If we remove the first item in the list
    Task temp = head;
    head = head.next;
    temp = null;
    size--;
    return;
  }

  Task previous = null;
  Task current = head;
  int i = 0;
  //Go to the selected index
  while (current != null && i < index) {
```

```
      previous = current;
      current = current.next;
      i++;
    }

    if (current == null) {
      System.out.println("Index out of bounds.");
      return;
    }

    previous.next = current.next;
    current = null;
    size--;
  }
```
Listing 5-5: TodoList.java

The argument to the method is the index of the entry inside the linked list, as it is presented during task listing in the console. As we will see in the next snippet, we start listing the tasks from number 1, which is something that we take into account in the calculations above.

Here is the code for the task listing:

```
public void displayTasks() {
  Task temp = head;
  int i = 1;
  while (temp != null) {
    System.out.println(i++ + ") Description: " + temp.description
        + ", Priority: " + temp.priority);
    temp = temp.next;
  }
}
```
Listing 5-6: TodoList.java

Finally, we present the code for the sorting of tasks according to their priority:

```
public void sortTasks() {
  int swapped;
  Task ptr1;
  Task ptr2 = null;

  if (head == null)
    return;

  do {
    swapped = 0; // will change if swapping happens
    ptr1 = head;

    while (ptr1.next != ptr2) {
      //Swap data of adjacent nodes
      if (ptr1.priority > ptr1.next.priority) {
        int tempPriority = ptr1.priority;
```

```
                ptr1.priority = ptr1.next.priority;
                ptr1.next.priority = tempPriority;

                String tempDescription = ptr1.description;
                ptr1.description = ptr1.next.description;
                ptr1.next.description = tempDescription;

                swapped = 1; //swap happened in this loop pass; don't stop yet
            }
            ptr1 = ptr1.next;
        }
        ptr2 = ptr1;
    } while (swapped != 0); //quit loop when no swap happened
  }
}
```

Listing 5-7: TodoList.java

The code employs the *bubble sort* algorithm to perform the task sorting operation. In bubble sort, we perform multiple passes of the linked list. Each time we find a task that has lower priority than its next task, then we perform swapping of those adjacent tasks. Over time, all entries will be sorted according to priority and there will eventually be a loop pass where no swapping will occur. This is when the algorithm will end.

You can find this project in GitHub:

https://github.com/htset/java_exercises_dsa/tree/master/Todo

6. Songs List

Let's create a simple program that takes an array of songs and sorts them by artist, album or release date, using *insertion sort*.

Proposed Solution

The Song class will contain information about the title of the song, the artist, the album and the release year:

```java
package Songs;

public class Song {
  public String title;
  public String artist;
  public String album;
  public int releaseYear;

  public Song(String title, String artist, String album, int releaseYear) {
    this.title = title;
    this.artist = artist;
    this.album = album;
    this.releaseYear = releaseYear;
  }
}
```

Listing 6-1: Song.java

Next, we define three methods, that will be used for the comparisons:

```java
package Songs;
import java.util.Comparator;

public class Songs {

  //Compare songs based on artist
  public static int compareByArtist(Song a, Song b) {
    return a.artist.compareTo(b.artist);
  }

  //Compare songs based on album
  public static int compareByAlbum(Song a, Song b) {
    return a.album.compareTo(b.album);
  }

  //Compare songs based on release date
  public static int compareByReleaseDate(Song a, Song b) {
    return a.releaseYear - b.releaseYear;
  }

  ...
```

Listing 6-2: Songs.java

In the first two methods, we compare two strings, while in the third one we compare two integers. Those methods will be used by the `insertionSort()` method:

```java
public static void insertionSort(Song[] arr, Comparator<Song> comparator) {
    for (int i = 1; i < arr.length; i++) {
        Song key = arr[i];
        int j = i - 1;

        //Move elements of arr[0..i-1], that are greater than key,
        //to one position ahead of their current position
        while (j >= 0 && comparator.compare(arr[j], key) > 0) {
            arr[j + 1] = arr[j];
            j = j - 1;
        }
        arr[j + 1] = key;
    }
}
```

Listing 6-3: Songs.java

We use the `Comparator` interface in order to use one of the 3 static methods that we defined earlier. This interface is then used as a parameter for the `insertionSort()` method to specify the comparison logic for sorting the `Song` array.

For instance, if we call `insertionSort()` like this:

```java
insertionSort(songs, Songs::compareByArtist);
```

then, the following code inside `insertionSort()`:

```java
while (j >= 0 && comparator.compare(arr[j], key) > 0)
```

will result in calling the `compareByArtist()` method. In this way, we don't have to write `insertionSort()` three times to accommodate for the three different types of comparison.

Note that we are essentially using a Lambda Expression with a reference to a static method. We could do this in a more traditional way, by creating three classes that implement the Comparator interface, like the following:

```java
//Comparator class for comparing songs by artist
class CompareByArtist implements Comparator<Song> {
    @Override
    public int compare(Song a, Song b) {
        return a.artist.compareTo(b.artist);
    }
}
```

Listing 6-4: Songs.java

Then we would call insertionSort() like this:

```
insertionSort(songs, new CompareByArtist());
```

Insertion sort works by taking each element in the array and moving it to the left part of the array in a sorted position. At any time, the left part of the array is sorted, while we take items from the right part. As we move an element to a place in the array, all the items to the right will have to move one place to the right.

This is all illustrated in the main() method where we call insertionSort() three times, each time passing a different comparison method. Each time, the array is sorted in a different way:

```java
public static void main(String[] args) {
  Song[] songs = {
      new Song("Song1", "Artist2", "Album1", 2010),
      new Song("Song2", "Artist1", "Album2", 2005),
      new Song("Song3", "Artist3", "Album1", 2015),
      new Song("Song4", "Artist4", "Album3", 2008),
      new Song("Song5", "Artist1", "Album2", 2003),
      new Song("Song6", "Artist3", "Album4", 2019),
      new Song("Song7", "Artist2", "Album3", 2012),
      new Song("Song8", "Artist4", "Album4", 2017),
      new Song("Song9", "Artist5", "Album5", 2014),
      new Song("Song10", "Artist5", "Album5", 2011)
  };

  //Sort by artist
  insertionSort(songs, Songs::compareByArtist);
  System.out.println("Sorted by Artist:");
  for (Song song : songs) {
    System.out.println(song.title + " from " + song.artist);
  }
  System.out.println();

  //Sort by album
  insertionSort(songs, Songs::compareByAlbum);
  System.out.println("Sorted by Album:");
  for (Song song : songs) {
    System.out.println(song.title + " from " + song.album);
  }
  System.out.println();

  //Sort by release date
  insertionSort(songs, Songs::compareByReleaseDate);
  System.out.println("Sorted by Release Date:");
  for (Song song : songs) {
    System.out.println(song.title + " released in " + song.releaseYear);
  }
  }
}
```

Listing 6-5: Songs.java

You can find this project in GitHub:

https://github.com/htset/java_exercises_dsa/tree/master/Songs

7. Task allocation

We will create a program where users can enter the description of tasks and their durations. The tasks will be allocated to workers, based on the amount of work that they already have taken over. This means that the task will be allocated to the worker with the lower workload.

Proposed Solution

We will use a *priority queue* to express the differences in priority between the various workers, based on their workload so far.

Let's first define the Task and Worker classes:

```java
package TaskAllocation;

public class Task {
  public String description;
  public int duration;

  public Task(String description, int duration) {
    this.description = description;
    this.duration = duration;
  }
}
```
Listing 7-1: Task.java

The Task class consists of the task description and duration in minutes.

```java
package TaskAllocation;

public class Worker {
  public int id;
  public int workload;

  public Worker(int id, int workload) {
    this.id = id;
    this.workload = workload;
  }
}
```
Listing 7-2: Worker.java

The Worker class contains the ID of the worker as well as the workload (also in minutes).

Next, we define the main() method:

```java
package TaskAllocation;
import java.util.ArrayList;
import java.util.Comparator;
import java.util.List;
import java.util.PriorityQueue;
```

```java
import java.util.Scanner;

public class TaskAllocation {
  public static void main(String[] args) {
    Scanner scanner = new Scanner(System.in);
    List<Task> tasks = new ArrayList<>();
    PriorityQueue<Worker> workerQueue
        = new PriorityQueue<>(Comparator.comparingInt(w -> w.workload));

    System.out.print("Enter the number of workers: ");
    int numWorkers = scanner.nextInt();

    //Initialize workers with ID and 0 workload
    for (int i = 0; i < numWorkers; i++) {
      workerQueue.add(new Worker(i, 0));
    }

    int choice;
    do {
      System.out.println("\nMenu:");
      System.out.println("1. Add Task");
      System.out.println("2. Display Tasks");
      System.out.println("3. Print Workers Queue");
      System.out.println("4. Exit");
      System.out.print("Enter your choice: ");
      choice = scanner.nextInt();

      switch (choice) {
        case 1:
          addTask(workerQueue, tasks, scanner);
          break;
        case 2:
          displayTasks(tasks);
          break;
        case 3:
          printWorkersQueue(workerQueue);
          break;
        case 4:
          System.out.println("Exiting program...");
          break;
        default:
          System.out.println("Invalid choice! Please try again.");
          break;
      }
    } while (choice != 4);

    scanner.close();
  }

  ...
```

Listing 7-3: TaskAllocation.java

The `main()` method displays the menu and gets the user's selections. It also initializes a list that will store the tasks, and a priority queue that will contain the workers.

Also note that when the program starts, the users should select the total number of workers; the workers will be subsequently referred to by their ID.

Next, we implement the method that adds a new task to the system:

```
//Method to add a task and allocate it to a worker
static void addTask(PriorityQueue<Worker> workerQueue,
                   List<Task> tasks, Scanner scanner) {
  System.out.print("Enter task description: ");
  String description = scanner.next();
  System.out.print("Enter task duration (in minutes): ");
  int duration = scanner.nextInt();

  if (workerQueue.size() == 0) {
    System.out.println("No workers available! Task cannot be assigned.");
    return;
  }

  //Dequeue the worker with the shortest workload
  Worker worker = workerQueue.poll();

  //Assign the task to the worker and update workload
  tasks.add(new Task(description, duration));
  System.out.println("Task added successfully and allocated to Worker "
      + worker.id + "!");

  //Update workload
  worker.workload += duration;

  //Store updated worker back to queue
  workerQueue.add(worker);
}
```

Listing 7-4: TaskAllocation.java

In order to find the worker that has the lowest workload, we store workers in the priority queue. Note that we are using the `workload` property as the parameter that will be used to sort the priority queue. This is specified in the definition of the queue in `main()`:

```
PriorityQueue<Worker> workerQueue
    = new PriorityQueue<>(Comparator.comparingInt(w -> w.workload));
```

When we dequeue an item from the queue, then we will get the item with lowest workload.

In `addTask()`, we get the worker with the lowest workload (the one that is positioned at the front of the queue) and we add the task's workload to the worker's own workload. Then, we store the task into the tasks list. Finally, the worker is inserted into the queue again; now the worker will be positioned according to the newly updated workload.

Finally, we present the code for two other operations, displaying the tasks and the workers information respectively:

```java
//Method to display all tasks
static void displayTasks(List<Task> tasks) {
  System.out.println("Task List:");
  for (Task task : tasks) {
    System.out.println("Task description: " + task.description
        + ", Duration: " + task.duration + " minutes");
  }
}

//Method to print the workers queue
static void printWorkersQueue(PriorityQueue<Worker> workerQueue) {
  System.out.println("Workers Queue:");
  for (Worker item : workerQueue) {
    System.out.println("Worker ID: " + item.id + ", Workload: "
        + item.workload + " minutes");
  }
 }
}
```

Listing 7-5: TaskAllocation.java

Note that traversing the priority queue will give us an *unordered* workers list. Apparently, this is the only way to get the contents of a priority queue, without dequeueing each element.

You can find this project in GitHub:

https://github.com/htset/java_exercises_dsa/tree/master/TaskAllocation

8. Word Frequencies

We will create a simple program that will parse a text file and will find the frequencies of all the words that appear in it.

Proposed Solution

This project is a use case for a dictionary structure. We will use a `HashMap` class that will store word and word frequency pairs.

Here is the program code:

```java
package WordFrequencies;
import java.io.BufferedReader;
import java.io.FileReader;
import java.io.IOException;
import java.util.HashMap;
import java.util.Map;

public class WordFrequencies {

  static String cleanWord(String word) {
    return new String(word
        .chars()
        .filter(Character::isLetter)
        .map(Character::toLowerCase)
        .toArray(), 0, (int) word.chars().filter(Character::isLetter).count());
  }

  public static void main(String[] args) {
    Map<String, Integer> wordFrequency = new HashMap<>();

    //Read text from file
    try (BufferedReader inputFile
            = new BufferedReader(new FileReader("input.txt"))) {
      String line;
      while ((line = inputFile.readLine()) != null) {
        for (String word : line.split(" ")) {
          String cleanedWord = cleanWord(word);
          if (!cleanedWord.isEmpty()) {
            wordFrequency.put(cleanedWord,
                wordFrequency.getOrDefault(cleanedWord, 0) + 1);
          }
        }
      }
    } catch (IOException e) {
      e.printStackTrace();
    }

    //Display word frequencies
    System.out.println("Word Frequencies:");
    wordFrequency.forEach((key, value)
        -> System.out.println(key + ": " + value));
  }
}
```

}

Listing 8-1: WordFrequencies.java

By using a `BufferedReader` object, we are reading the input file, line by line. Then, we split each line, based on spaces and we process each word to make it lowercase and remove non-letter characters. This processing is performed by the `cleanWord()` method, that takes a string, breaks it into characters, then filters the characters to keep only letters and numbers. Finally, it maps each character into lowercase ones and creates a new string based on them.

Then, we add the word in the `HashMap`. If the word does not already exist in the `HashMap`, then `getOrDefault()` will return zero, otherwise it will return its frequency so far.

Finally, we employ a `forEach()` loop to print all the words and their frequencies to the console. Note the use of a *lambda function* as argument to `forEach()`.

You can find this project in GitHub:

https://github.com/htset/java_exercises_dsa/tree/master/WordFrequencies

9. Syntax Checker

Let's create a trivial syntax checker that will scan a source code file and will determine whether the parentheses, brackets, or braces in the code are balanced or not.

Proposed Solution

In source code, when we open a series of parentheses, brackets, or braces, we have to make sure that they are closed in the reverse order.

The fact that items entered in a *stack* are extracted in the reverse order, makes it suitable for this algorithm:

```
package SyntaxChecker;

public class Stack {
  private char[] items;
  private int top;

  ...
```
Listing 9-1: Stack.java

Here is the code for the stack initialization:

```
public Stack() {
  items = new char[100];
  top = -1;
}
```
Listing 9-2: Stack.java

Next, we add the code for stack *push* and *pop*, as well as a method to check if the stack is empty:

```
public void push(char c) {
  if (top == items.length - 1) {
    System.out.println("Stack is full");
    System.exit(1);
  }
  items[++top] = c;
}

public char pop() {
  if (top == -1) {
    System.out.println("Stack is empty");
    System.exit(1);
  }
  return items[top--];
}

public boolean isEmpty() {
  return (top == -1);
```

    }
}

Listing 9-3: Stack.java

The most interesting part of the code is the algorithm that checks whether the file is balanced or not:

```java
package SyntaxChecker;

import java.io.BufferedReader;
import java.io.InputStreamReader;
import java.io.FileReader;
import java.io.IOException;

public class SyntaxChecker {
  static int checkBalanced(String filename) {
    try (BufferedReader file = new BufferedReader(new FileReader(filename))) {
      int c;
      Stack stack = new Stack();

      while ((c = file.read()) != -1) {
        char ch = (char) c; //read() returns an int
        if (ch == '(' || ch == '[' || ch == '{') {
          stack.push(ch);
        } else if (ch == ')' || ch == ']' || ch == '}') {
          if (stack.isEmpty()) {
            return 0;
          }

          char openingChar = stack.pop();

          if ((ch == ')' && openingChar != '(') ||
              (ch == ']' && openingChar != '[') ||
              (ch == '}' && openingChar != '{')) {
            return 0;
          }
        }
      }

      return stack.isEmpty() ? 1 : 0;
    } catch (IOException e) {
      e.printStackTrace();
      return 0;
    }
  }

  public static void main(String[] args) {
    try (BufferedReader reader
            = new BufferedReader(new InputStreamReader(System.in))) {
      System.out.print("Path to the source file: ");
      String filename = reader.readLine();

      if (checkBalanced(filename) == 1) {
```

```
            System.out.println("The input file is balanced.");
        } else {
            System.out.println("The input file is not balanced.");
        }
    } catch (IOException e) {
      e.printStackTrace();
    }
  }
}
```

Listing 9-4: SyntaxChecker.java

We open and parse the source code file, and we push the bracket *opening* characters into the stack. When we encounter a *closing* character, then we pop the first available opening character from the stack.

If there is a mismatch between those two characters, we conclude that the file is not balanced. At the end, we also check that the stack is emptied; if not, then the file is still unbalanced.

Note that this is a trivial version of the algorithm. In fact, if we try to check the exercises's own source file (*SyntaxChecker.java*) for parentheses balancing, we will get an error – even though the code compiles. That's because we use single characters (opening or closing) in our code during checking, like in the following line:

```
if (c == '(' || c == '[' || c == '{')
```

A more advanced version of the algorithm would not take those characters (e.g. those enclosed in quotes) into account.

You can find this project in GitHub:

https://github.com/htset/java_exercises_dsa/tree/master/SyntaxChecker

10. Maze Solver

In this exercise, we will use a *stack* to find our way through a maze.

Proposed Solution

We will define a maze as a two-dimensional array of integers. The walls will be marked with ones (1), while the corridors of the maze will be marked with zeroes (0).

Below, we can see the definition of a 15x15 maze:

```java
private int[][] matrix = {
    {0, 1, 0, 0, 0, 0, 0, 0, 0, 0, 0, 0, 0, 0, 0},
    {0, 1, 0, 1, 0, 1, 1, 1, 1, 0, 1, 1, 1, 1, 0},
    {0, 1, 0, 1, 0, 1, 0, 0, 0, 0, 1, 0, 0, 0, 0},
    {0, 0, 0, 1, 0, 1, 0, 1, 1, 1, 1, 0, 1, 1, 0},
    {0, 1, 0, 1, 0, 1, 0, 0, 0, 0, 1, 0, 1, 0, 0},
    {0, 1, 0, 1, 0, 1, 1, 1, 1, 0, 1, 0, 1, 1, 0},
    {0, 1, 0, 1, 0, 0, 0, 0, 1, 0, 1, 0, 0, 0, 0},
    {0, 1, 0, 1, 1, 1, 1, 0, 1, 0, 1, 0, 1, 1, 0},
    {0, 1, 0, 0, 0, 0, 1, 0, 1, 0, 1, 0, 0, 1, 0},
    {0, 1, 1, 1, 1, 0, 1, 0, 1, 0, 1, 0, 1, 1, 0},
    {0, 0, 0, 0, 1, 0, 1, 0, 1, 0, 1, 0, 0, 0, 0},
    {0, 1, 1, 0, 1, 0, 1, 0, 1, 0, 1, 1, 1, 1, 0},
    {0, 0, 1, 0, 1, 0, 0, 0, 1, 0, 0, 0, 0, 1, 0},
    {0, 1, 1, 1, 1, 1, 1, 1, 1, 1, 1, 0, 1, 0},
    {0, 0, 0, 0, 0, 0, 0, 0, 0, 0, 0, 0, 0, 1, 0}
};
```

Listing 10-1: MazeSolver.java

The entrance of the maze is at the top left corner, and the exit at the bottom right corner.

We will use a stack structure to solve this maze. As we move through the maze, we store the entered point coordinates in the stack. When we reach a dead end, then we will have to backtrack, and we will do this by popping one point from the stack. This algorithm is called *Depth-first search (DFS)*, as it goes inside the maze as deep as possible, only to go back and try another direction when no way is found.

Here is the code for the coordinate points:

```java
package MazeSolver;

public class Point {
  public int row, col;

  public Point() {
    row = 0;
    col = 0;
  }

  public Point(int x, int y) {
    row = x;
```

```
    col = y;
  }
}
```
Listing 10-2: Point.java

And here is the code for the stack:

```
package MazeSolver;

public class Stack<T> {
  private T[] items;
  private int top;

  public Stack(int capacity) {
    items = (T[]) new Object[capacity];
    top = -1;
  }

  public boolean isEmpty() {
    return top == -1;
  }

  public void push(T t) {
    top++;
    items[top] = t;
  }

  public T pop() {
    return items[top--];
  }
}
```
Listing 10-3: Stack.java

To make it more interesting, we have created a stack using *Java generics*. The stack will eventually contain an array of point coordinates. We have defined methods to initialize the stack, to check if it's empty, as well as to push and pop objects in the stack.

Note that we keep it simple and don't include bounds checking, as we will instantiate a stack with the maximum capacity needed to solve the maze (*ROWS*COLS*).

Now, it is time to introduce a class that will handle the maze:

```java
package MazeSolver;

public class Maze {
    private Stack<Point> stack = new Stack<>(ROWS * COLS);

    private static final int ROWS = 15;
    private static final int COLS = 15;
    private int[][] matrix = {
        {0, 1, 0, 0, 0, 0, 0, 0, 0, 0, 0, 0, 0, 0, 0},
        {0, 1, 0, 1, 0, 1, 1, 1, 1, 0, 1, 1, 1, 1, 0},
        {0, 1, 0, 1, 0, 1, 0, 0, 0, 0, 1, 0, 0, 0, 0},
        {0, 0, 0, 1, 0, 1, 0, 1, 1, 1, 1, 0, 1, 1, 0},
        {0, 1, 0, 1, 0, 1, 0, 0, 0, 0, 1, 0, 1, 0, 0},
        {0, 1, 0, 1, 0, 1, 1, 1, 1, 0, 1, 0, 1, 1, 0},
        {0, 1, 0, 1, 0, 0, 0, 0, 1, 0, 1, 0, 0, 0, 0},
        {0, 1, 0, 1, 1, 1, 1, 0, 1, 0, 1, 0, 1, 1, 0},
        {0, 1, 0, 0, 0, 0, 1, 0, 1, 0, 1, 0, 0, 1, 0},
        {0, 1, 1, 1, 1, 0, 1, 0, 1, 0, 1, 0, 1, 1, 0},
        {0, 0, 0, 0, 1, 0, 1, 0, 1, 0, 1, 0, 0, 0, 0},
        {0, 1, 1, 0, 1, 0, 1, 0, 1, 0, 1, 1, 1, 1, 0},
        {0, 0, 1, 0, 1, 0, 0, 0, 1, 0, 0, 0, 0, 1, 0},
        {0, 1, 1, 1, 1, 1, 1, 1, 1, 1, 1, 0, 1, 0},
        {0, 0, 0, 0, 0, 0, 0, 0, 0, 0, 0, 0, 0, 1, 0}
    };

    public Maze() { }

    ...
```

Listing 10-4: Maze.java

Next, we add the code to check whether we can move to a cell:

```java
//Check if we can move to this cell
private boolean canMove(int row, int col) {
    return (row >= 0
        && row < ROWS
        && col >= 0
        && col < COLS
        && matrix[row][col] == 0);
}
```

Listing 10-5: Maze.java

The cell must me within the maze bounds and should be part of a corridor.

We also provide a method to print the maze:

```java
public void print() {
    for (int i = 0; i < ROWS; i++) {
        for (int j = 0; j < COLS; j++) {
            System.out.print(matrix[i][j] + " ");
        }
        System.out.println();
    }
```

```
}
```
Listing 10-6: Maze.java

The following method implements the maze solving algorithm:

```java
//Solve the maze using backtracking
public int solve(int row, int col) {
  if (row == ROWS - 1 && col == COLS - 1) {
    //destination reached
    stack.push(new Point(row, col));
    return 1;
  }

  if (canMove(row, col)) {
    stack.push(new Point(row, col));
    matrix[row][col] = 2; //Mark visited

    //Move right
    if (solve(row, col + 1) == 1)
      return 1;

    //Move down
    if (solve(row + 1, col) == 1)
      return 1;

    //Move left
    if (solve(row, col - 1) == 1)
      return 1;

    //Move up
    if (solve(row - 1, col) == 1)
      return 1;

    //If none of the above movements work, backtrack
    stack.pop();
    return 0;
  }

  return 0;
}
```
Listing 10-7: Maze.java

First of all, we check whether the destination has been reached, by comparing the current row and column with the constant values ROWS and COLS.

In the opposite case, we first check if we can actually move to this cell, i.e., if it is part of a corridor and is within the maze bounds. If so, we add its coordinates into the stack and we mark the cell with the number 2, to mark the fact that we have already passed from this cell.

Then, we proceed with calling recursively the solve() method for all four directions, starting with right and down, and then trying with left and up. If none of those movements results in solving the maze (i.e. they all return 0), then we will have to backtrack. Since this point in the maze was not eventually part of the solution, we pop it from the stack.

We also define a method to print the path followed to solve the maze. We get it by popping the visited cells of the maze from the stack, one by one:

```java
  public void printPath() {
    while (!stack.isEmpty()) {
      Point p = stack.pop();
      System.out.print("(" + p.row + ", " + p.col + "), ");
    }
  }
}
```

Listing 10-8: Maze.java

Finally, let's see the main method of the program:

```java
package MazeSolver;

public class MazeSolver {
  public static void main(String[] args) {
    Maze maze = new Maze();

    System.out.println("This is the maze:");
    maze.print();

    if (maze.solve(0, 0) == 1) {
      System.out.println("\n\nThis is the path found:");
      maze.printPath();

      System.out.println("\n\nThis is the maze with all the points crossed:");
      maze.print();
    } else {
      System.out.println("No path found");
    }
  }
}
```

Listing 10-9: MazeSolver.java

We first print the initial maze, then we solve the maze. Next, we print the solution path. Finally, we display the map once more; all the points that we crossed during our search will be marked with '2'.

You can find this project in GitHub:

https://github.com/htset/java_exercises_dsa/tree/master/MazeSolver

11. File Indexer

For this exercise, we will create a program that will recursively index all the files in a specified folder. The information about the indexed files (filename and location in the disk) will be stored in a *Binary Search Tree (BST)* for faster searching.

Proposed Solution

The Binary Search Tree structure is a tree where each node has only two children, left and right. Here is the definition of the class:

```java
package FileIndexer;

import java.io.*;
import java.nio.file.*;
import java.util.Scanner;

class FileIndexer {
  private class Node {
    public String fileName;
    public String filePath;
    public Node left;
    public Node right;

    public Node(String name, String path) {
      fileName = name;
      filePath = path;
      left = null;
      right = null;
    }
  }

  private Node root;

  ...
```

Listing 11-1: FileIndexer.java

Each node of the tree contains two strings, the file name and the file location. It also contains references to the two children nodes.

Next, we define a method to insert a new node into the tree:

```java
  //Insert node to tree
  private void insertNode(String fileName, String filePath) {
    //If the tree is empty, insert node here
    if (root == null) {
      root = new Node(fileName, filePath);
      return;
    }

    //If not empty, then go down the tree
    Node current = root;
```

```java
      while (true) {
        if (fileName.compareTo(current.fileName) < 0) {
          if (current.left == null) {
            current.left = new Node(fileName, filePath);
            return;
          }
          current = current.left;
        } else {
          if (current.right == null) {
            current.right = new Node(fileName, filePath);
            return;
          }
          current = current.right;
        }
      }
    }
  }
```

Listing 11-2: FileIndexer.java

Starting from the root of the tree, we move downwards to the left or to the right depending on the inserted value.

Next, we define the method that will recursively index all files into the tree:

```java
//Index the specified directory
private void indexDirectoryHelper(String dirPath) {
  //If it's not a directory, return
  if (!Files.isDirectory(Paths.get(dirPath)))
    return;

  //Loop over files within directory
  try (DirectoryStream<Path> stream
    = Files.newDirectoryStream(Paths.get(dirPath))) {
    for (Path entry : stream) {
      if (Files.isRegularFile(entry)) {
        String fileName = entry.getFileName().toString();
        insertNode(fileName, entry.toString());
      }
    }
  } catch (IOException e) {
    e.printStackTrace();
  }

  //Loop over directories within directory
  try (DirectoryStream<Path> stream
    = Files.newDirectoryStream(Paths.get(dirPath))) {
    for (Path entry : stream) {
      if (Files.isDirectory(entry)) {
        //Recursive indexing
        indexDirectoryHelper(entry.toString());
      }
    }
  } catch (IOException e) {
    e.printStackTrace();
```

```
    }
  }
```

Listing 11-3: FileIndexer.java

We use the `java.nio.file` package methods to check if a path exists and corresponds to a directory (`Files.isDirectory`). We then loop over all the files inside the directory, one by one, and we insert them in the tree as new nodes.

Then, we loop over the directories and also index them recursively.

Next, we define a method to recursively delete the nodes of the tree:

```
//Deallocate memory recursively
private void deleteSubtree(Node root) {
  if (root != null) {
    deleteSubtree(root.left);
    deleteSubtree(root.right);
    root = null;
  }
}
```

Listing 11-4: FileIndexer.java

We perform this by setting the root of the subtree to null, so that the subtree will be removed by the garbage collector.

Then, we have the directory traversal method (also recursive):

```
private void traverse(Node root) {
  if (root != null) {
    traverse(root.left);
    System.out.println(root.fileName + ": " + root.filePath);
    traverse(root.right);
  }
}
```

Listing 11-5: FileIndexer.java

Now, we turn to the *public* interface provided by the `FileIndexer` class (note that all method until now were `private`).

We define methods to index and print all the files in a directory. Those methods call the respective private helper methods:

```
public void indexDirectory(String directoryPath) {
  root = null;
  indexDirectoryHelper(directoryPath);
}

public void printFiles() {
  System.out.println("Indexed files:");
  traverse(root);
```

```
}
```
Listing 11-6: FileIndexer.java

After the tree has been set up, we can call method `searchFileLocation()` to get the location of a file:

```java
//Search for a file in the BST
public String searchFileLocation(String filename) {
  //Traverse the tree until a match is found or the tree is exhausted
  Node current = root;
  while (current != null) {
    if (filename.equals(current.fileName)) {
      return current.filePath; //File found
    } else if (filename.compareTo(current.fileName) < 0) {
      current = current.left; //Search in the left subtree
    } else {
      current = current.right; //Search in the right subtree
    }
  }
  return ""; //File not found
}
```
Listing 11-7: FileIndexer.java

We traverse the tree until we find a node with the specified file name. If the tree is exhausted, then we return null.

Finally, here is the `main()` method:

```java
public static void main(String[] args) {
  Scanner scanner = new Scanner(System.in);

  System.out.print("Path to index recursively: ");
  String path = scanner.nextLine();

  FileIndexer indexer = new FileIndexer();
  indexer.indexDirectory(path);
  indexer.printFiles();

  System.out.print("Let's search for a file's location. Give the file name: ");
  String filenameToSearch = scanner.nextLine();

  String location = indexer.searchFileLocation(filenameToSearch);
  if (!location.isEmpty()) {
    System.out.println("File " + filenameToSearch
        + " found. Location: " + location);
  } else {
    System.out.println("File " + filenameToSearch + " not found.");
  }

  scanner.close();
 }
}
```

Listing 11-8: FileIndexer.java

Users can index the contents of a folder and then they can search for a specific filename.

You can find this project in GitHub:

https://github.com/htset/java_exercises_dsa/tree/master/FileIndexer

12. Inventory with AVL Tree

In this exercise, we will create an inventory program, that will store information about the company's products in an AVL tree structure.

Proposed Solution

An *AVL (Adelson-Velsky and Landis) tree* is a *self-balancing* binary search tree structure. With the term *balanced*, we mean that both branches of the tree have the same depth or differ by one level at the most. To achieve this, a process called *rebalancing* is occasionally performed, that changes the tree structure in way that the tree is closer to be balanced.

The AVL tree has almost the same structure as a simple binary search tree (BST); the difference lies in the rebalancing algorithm. Let's see the structure:

```java
package Inventory;

import java.util.Random;

class Product {
  public int id;
  public String name;
  public float price;
  public int quantity;
}

class InventoryNode {
  public Product product;
  public InventoryNode left;
  public InventoryNode right;
  public int height;
}
```

Listing 12-1: Inventory.java

The `InventoryNode` class contains a product object and two references to the tree's branches. Most importantly, it also contains the `height` property, which is used to track the tree's height.

Next, we define the `Inventory` class, which contains a reference that is the root of the AVL tree. We also define two internal methods of the tree:

```java
class Inventory {
  private InventoryNode root;

  private int getHeight(InventoryNode node) {
    return node == null ? 0 : node.height;
  }

  private int getBalance(InventoryNode node) {
    return node == null ? 0 : getHeight(node.left) - getHeight(node.right);
  }
```

Listing 12-2: Inventory.java

The former gives us the height of the tree, while the latter checks whether the tree is balanced or not.

Afterwards, we add code for the creation of a new node in the tree:

```java
//Create a new node with the given product
private InventoryNode newNode(Product product) {
    InventoryNode node = new InventoryNode();
    node.product = product;
    node.left = null;
    node.right = null;
    node.height = 1;
    return node;
}
```

Listing 12-3: Inventory.java

Note that the height of the node is set to 1.

Next, we proceed with the definition of two methods for the rotation of the tree to the left or to the right:

```java
//Right rotate subtree
private InventoryNode rotateRight(InventoryNode y) {
    InventoryNode x = y.left;
    InventoryNode T2 = x.right;

    //Perform rotation
    x.right = y;
    y.left = T2;

    //Update heights
    y.height = Math.max(getHeight(y.left), getHeight(y.right)) + 1;
    x.height = Math.max(getHeight(x.left), getHeight(x.right)) + 1;

    //Return new root
    return x;
}

//Left rotate subtree
private InventoryNode rotateLeft(InventoryNode x) {
    InventoryNode y = x.right;
    InventoryNode T2 = y.left;

    //Perform rotation
    y.left = x;
    x.right = T2;

    //Update heights
    x.height = Math.max(getHeight(x.left), getHeight(x.right)) + 1;
    y.height = Math.max(getHeight(y.left), getHeight(y.right)) + 1;
```

```java
  //Return new root
  return y;
}
```

Listing 12-4: Inventory.java

Those two methods will be used when we will try to insert a new node into the tree:

```java
//Insert a product in the AVL tree
private InventoryNode insertProduct(InventoryNode node, Product product) {
  if (node == null)
    return newNode(product);

  //Insert the product
  if (product.id < node.product.id)
    node.left = insertProduct(node.left, product);
  else if (product.id > node.product.id)
    node.right = insertProduct(node.right, product);
  else
    return node; //Duplicate IDs not allowed

  //Update height of this node
  node.height = 1 + Math.max(getHeight(node.left), getHeight(node.right));

  //Get balance factor
  int balance = getBalance(node);

  //Left Left Case
  if (balance > 1 && product.id < node.left.product.id)
    return rotateRight(node);

  //Right Right Case
  if (balance < -1 && product.id > node.right.product.id)
    return rotateLeft(node);

  //Left Right Case
  if (balance > 1 && product.id > node.left.product.id) {
    node.left = rotateLeft(node.left);
    return rotateRight(node);
  }

  //Right Left Case
  if (balance < -1 && product.id < node.right.product.id) {
    node.right = rotateRight(node.right);
    return rotateLeft(node);
  }

  return node;
}
```

Listing 12-5: Inventory.java

The idea here is to check for the tree balance after inserting a new node to it. If the tree becomes unbalanced, then we will have to rotate it either to the left or to the right.

Next, we present the methods to traverse the tree while printing its contents, as well as the code to search for a specific product in the tree:

```java
private void traverseTree(InventoryNode node) {
  if (node != null) {
    traverseTree(node.left);
    System.out.println("ID: " + node.product.id + ", " +
        "Name: " + node.product.name + ", " +
        "Price: " + node.product.price + ", " +
        "Quantity: " + node.product.quantity);
    traverseTree(node.right);
  }
}

private InventoryNode searchProduct(InventoryNode node, int id) {
  if (node == null || node.product.id == id) {
    if (node == null)
      System.out.println("Product not found.");
    else
      System.out.println("Found product: ID: " + node.product.id + ", " +
          "Name: " + node.product.name + ", " +
          "Price: " + node.product.price + ", " +
          "Quantity: " + node.product.quantity);
    return node;
  }

  System.out.println("Visited product ID: " + node.product.id);

  if (id < node.product.id)
    return searchProduct(node.left, id);
  else
    return searchProduct(node.right, id);
}
```
Listing 12-6: Inventory.java

Traversing the tree means visiting each node in the tree, and this is performed recursively, first for the left branch and then for the right branch.

Searching for a product in the tree works in similar fashion: we visit a node, and we check the product's ID. If it matches the search ID, then we print the product details, and the method returns. Otherwise, we visit the left or the right branch of the tree recursively, depending on the search ID.

All the methods we have defined so far are private. We also define three public methods that will call those private methods:

```java
public void insertProduct(Product product) {
  root = insertProduct(root, product);
```

```
}
public void traverseTree() {
  traverseTree(root);
}

public InventoryNode searchProduct(int id) {
  return searchProduct(root, id);
}
```

Listing 12-7: Inventory.java

We use this convention because the respective private methods with the same name (insertProduct, traverseTree and searchProduct) are called recursively. In this way, we provide a clean interface to programmers that will use our code.

Finally, here is the main() method:

```
public static void main(String[] args) {
  Inventory inv = new Inventory();
  Product[] products = new Product[100];

  Random random = new Random();
  //Initialize products with random values
  for (int i = 0; i < 100; i++) {
    products[i] = new Product();
    products[i].id = i + 1;
    products[i].name = "Product " + (i + 1);
    products[i].price = random.nextFloat() * 100.0f;
    products[i].quantity = random.nextInt(100) + 1;
  }

  //Shuffle products array
  for (int i = 99; i >= 0; i--) {
    int j = random.nextInt(i + 1);
    Product temp = products[i];
    products[i] = products[j];
    products[j] = temp;
  }

  //Insert products into the inventory
  for (Product product : products) {
    inv.insertProduct(product);
  }

  //Display all products in the inventory
  System.out.println("Inventory:");
  inv.traverseTree();

  //Search for a specific product
  int productIdToSearch = 35;
  InventoryNode foundProduct = inv.searchProduct(productIdToSearch);
  if (foundProduct != null) {
    System.out.println("Product found: ID: " + foundProduct.product.id + ", " +
```

```
                "Name: " + foundProduct.product.name + ", " +
                "Price: " + foundProduct.product.price + ", " +
                "Quantity: " + foundProduct.product.quantity);
        } else {
            System.out.println("Product with ID " + productIdToSearch + " not found.");
        }
    }
}
```

Listing 12-8: Inventory.java

We create 100 products with random quantities and prices and place them in an array. Then we shuffle the array in a random order. Afterwards, we insert the products into the AVL tree, and we print its contents.

Finally, a search is performed for a specific product ID. During the search process we print the visited nodes to get an idea of how fast we will find the specific ID inside the AVL tree.

You can find this project in GitHub:

https://github.com/htset/java_exercises_dsa/tree/master/Inventory

13. Social Network

A social network is essentially a *graph* of nodes that depicts the users of the network along with their connections to their friends. In this exercise, we will create such a graph and we will implement the functionality to recommend new friends according to a user's current connections.

Proposed Solution

There are various ways to implement the users' graph, for example using *sparse two-dimensional matrices*. Here we will construct the graph with the use of a *one-dimensional array* of users, where the connections are stored in a linked list:

```java
package SocialNetwork;

class FriendNode {
  public String name;
  public FriendNode next;

  public FriendNode(String name) {
    this.name = name;
    this.next = null;
  }
}

class User {
  public String name;
  public FriendNode friends;

  public User(String name) {
    this.name = name;
    this.friends = null;
  }
}
```

Listing 13-1: SocialNetwork.java

The `User` class contains the name of the user as well as a linked list of the user's friends.

Next, we define a *queue* class that will be used by the friend recommendation algorithm. For learning purposes, we will make our own queue instead of using the one from `java.util` package:

```java
class MyQueue {
  private class QueueNode {
    public int userIndex;
    public QueueNode next;

    public QueueNode(int userIndex) {
      this.userIndex = userIndex;
      this.next = null;
    }
```

```java
  }

  private QueueNode front;
  private QueueNode rear;

  public MyQueue() {
    front = rear = null;
  }

  public boolean isEmpty() {
    return front == null;
  }

  public void enqueue(int userIndex) {
    QueueNode newNode = new QueueNode(userIndex);
    if (isEmpty()) {
      front = rear = newNode;
    } else {
      rear.next = newNode;
      rear = newNode;
    }
  }

  public int dequeue() {
    if (isEmpty()) {
      System.out.println("Queue is empty!");
      return -1;
    }

    int userIndex = front.userIndex;
    front = front.next;

    if (front == null) {
      rear = null;
    }

    return userIndex;
  }
}
```

Listing 13-2: SocialNetwork.java

The queue contains the indexes of the users, as they will appear inside the users' array (see below in the Graph class). We define the class for the queue nodes, and methods to enqueue and dequeue user indexes inside the queue, as well as to check whether it is empty or not.

Now, let's see how we will insert users into the graph and how we will define the connections with their friends. We define the Graph class, that essentially contains an array of all the users of the social network:

```java
class Graph {
  private static final int MAX_USERS = 100;
  private User[] users;
```

```
  private int numUsers;

  public Graph() {
    users = new User[MAX_USERS];
    numUsers = 0;
  }

  ...
```

Listing 13-3: SocialNetwork.java

Next, we provide the functionality to add a new user to the graph:

```
  public void addUser(String name) {
    if (numUsers >= MAX_USERS) {
      System.out.println("Max user limit reached!");
      return;
    }

    users[numUsers] = new User(name);
    numUsers++;
  }
```

Listing 13-4: SocialNetwork.java

We use the following method to add a new connection to a user:

```
  public void addConnection(int src, int dest) {
    if (src < 0 || src >= numUsers || dest < 0 || dest >= numUsers) {
      System.out.println("Invalid user index!");
      return;
    }

    //Add bidirectional connection
    FriendNode newFriendSrc = new FriendNode(users[dest].name);
    newFriendSrc.next = users[src].friends;
    users[src].friends = newFriendSrc;

    FriendNode newFriendDest = new FriendNode(users[src].name);
    newFriendDest.next = users[dest].friends;
    users[dest].friends = newFriendDest;
  }
```

Listing 13-5: SocialNetwork.java

Note that when we add a new connection, we make it bidirectional. That is, we insert a friend node for each one of the connection's ends.

Next, we proceed to the more interesting stuff, the recommender method:

```
  public void recommendFriends(int userIndex) {
    System.out.println("Recommended friends for " + users[userIndex].name + ":");

    //Store the indexes of the user's friends
    MyQueue queue = new MyQueue();
    //Store the persons that we have already visited
```

```java
      boolean[] visited = new boolean[MAX_USERS];

      visited[userIndex] = true;
      //Enqueue the starting user
      queue.enqueue(userIndex);

      while (!queue.isEmpty()) {
        int currentUserIndex = queue.dequeue();
        FriendNode current = users[currentUserIndex].friends;

        //Traverse the user's friends
        while (current != null) {
          int friendIndex = -1;
          //Find the friend's index
          for (int i = 0; i < numUsers; i++) {
            if (current.name.equals(users[i].name)) {
              friendIndex = i;
              break;
            }
          }

          //Check if the friend is already visited
          if (friendIndex != -1 && !visited[friendIndex]) {
            System.out.println("- " + current.name);
            //Add friend to visited array
            visited[friendIndex] = true;
            //Enqueue friend
            queue.enqueue(friendIndex);
          }

          //Move to the next friend
          current = current.next;
        }
      }
    }
  }
}
```

Listing 13-6: SocialNetwork.java

The `recommendFriends()` method uses *breadth-first search (BFS)* to traverse the social network graph, starting from the specified user and visiting all connected users to recommend friends. It marks users as visited (using the `visited[]` array) to avoid recommending the same friend multiple times and enqueues each friend to ensure all potential friends are discovered and recommended.

The BFS algorithm makes use of a queue, where we store the indexes of the user's friends as we follow the linked list. We then use the queue to get the friends of the user's friends, and in this way, we are able to travel through the connections of the graph and find all the connected people to the specific user.

Finally, here is the `main()` method:

```java
public class SocialNetwork {
  public static void main(String[] args) {
    Graph graph = new Graph();
    graph.addUser("User A");
    graph.addUser("User B");
    graph.addUser("User C");
    graph.addUser("User D");
    graph.addUser("User E");
    graph.addUser("User F");
    graph.addUser("User G");
    graph.addUser("User H");

    graph.addConnection(0, 1);
    graph.addConnection(1, 2);
    graph.addConnection(2, 3);
    graph.addConnection(4, 5);
    graph.addConnection(5, 7);
    graph.addConnection(3, 6);

    graph.recommendFriends(0);
    graph.recommendFriends(1);
    graph.recommendFriends(7);
  }
}
```

Listing 13-7: SocialNetwork.java

In main(), we add users to the graph and we enter their friend connections. Then we run the algorithm to get friend recommendations.

You can find this project in GitHub:

https://github.com/htset/java_exercises_dsa/tree/master/SocialNetwork

14. Flights

Let's create a console application that will maintain a list of flights between cities and that will find the best combination of flights in terms of ticket cost.

Proposed Solution

This problem involves creating a graph between the cities. This graph will be weighted, with the cost of the respective ticket. We will use *Dijkstra's algorithm* to find the cheapest path between two of those cities.

First, we define the `City` class that will store a map of the connected cities and the respective costs:

```java
package Flights;

import java.util.*;

public class Flights {

  //Structure to represent each city
  public static class City {
    public String name;
    public Map<String, Integer> flights;

    public City(String name) {
      this.name = name;
      this.flights = new HashMap<>();
    }
  }

  ...
```

Listing 14-1: Flights.java

Next, we define the `FlightGraph` class:

```java
  //Graph class to represent all cities and flights
  public static class FlightGraph {
    //Map of city names and their objects
    public Map<String, City> cities = new HashMap<>();

    ...
```

Listing 14-2: Flights.java

This class contains all the cities objects in a map along with their names. We can add cities and flights to our graph with the following methods:

```java
    //Add a city to the graph
    public void addCity(String name) {
      cities.put(name, new City(name));
    }
```

```java
//Add a flight between two cities and its cost
public void addFlight(String src, String dest, int cost) {
  //Assuming flights are bidirectional
  cities.get(src).flights.put(dest, cost);
  cities.get(dest).flights.put(src, cost);
}
```

Listing 14-3: Flights.java

Note that we assume that flights are bidirectional, and that they have the same price in both directions.

Next, we calculate the cheapest route between two cities using Dijkstra's algorithm:

```java
//Function to find the cheapest route between two cities
//using Dijkstra's algorithm
public List<String> findCheapestRoute(String src, String dest,
                                      Map<String, Integer> dist) {
  //Initialize the distance map and previous node map
  dist.clear();
  Map<String, String> prev = new HashMap<>();
  PriorityQueue<Map.Entry<String, Integer>> pq
      = new PriorityQueue<>(Map.Entry.comparingByValue());

  //Set all distances to infinity initially
  for (String city : cities.keySet()) {
    dist.put(city, Integer.MAX_VALUE);
    prev.put(city, null);
  }

  //Distance to the source is 0
  dist.put(src, 0);
  pq.offer(new AbstractMap.SimpleEntry<>(src, 0));

  //Main loop to process each node
  while (!pq.isEmpty()) {
    Map.Entry<String, Integer> entry = pq.poll();
    String u = entry.getKey();
    int uDist = entry.getValue();

    //Process each neighbor of the current node
    for (Map.Entry<String, Integer> flight : cities.get(u).flights.entrySet()) {
      String v = flight.getKey();
      int cost = flight.getValue();

      //If a shorter path to v is found
      if (dist.get(u) != Integer.MAX_VALUE && dist.get(u) + cost < dist.get(v)) {
        dist.put(v, dist.get(u) + cost);
        prev.put(v, u);
        pq.offer(new AbstractMap.SimpleEntry<>(v, dist.get(v)));
      }
    }
  }
```

```java
    //Reconstructing the path from source to destination
    List<String> path = new ArrayList<>();
    for (String at = dest; at != null; at = prev.get(at)) {
      path.add(at);
    }
    Collections.reverse(path);

    return path;
  }
```
Listing 14-4: Flights.java

Initially, we initialize a dictionary to store the distances from the source city to every other city, marking the source city's distance as 0 and all other cities as *infinity*. We use a priority queue to process cities based on their distance from the source, dequeuing the city with the shortest distance first.

For each dequeued city, we examine its neighboring cities, updating their distances if a shorter path through the current city is found. This process continues until all cities are visited or until the destination city is reached.

Upon completion, we reconstruct the shortest path from the source to the destination using the information stored in the previous node map, facilitating the determination of the total price of the route.

To avoid getting stuck in loops during the graph traversal, we keep track of the cities visited in the current path (`dist` map). If a city has already been visited in the current path, we skip exploring flights from that city to prevent loops.

We can calculate and print all the possible flights between two cities using *Depth-First Search (DFS)*:

```java
    //Display all possible flights between two cities using DFS
    public void displayAllFlights(String src, String dest) {
      if (!cities.containsKey(src) || !cities.containsKey(dest)) {
        System.out.println("Invalid cities entered.");
        return;
      }

      Set<String> visited = new HashSet<>();
      Stack<String> path = new Stack<>();
      path.push(src);
      dfs(src, dest, visited, path);
    }
```
Listing 14-5: Flights.java

We see that method `displayAllFlights()` calls the recursive `dfs()` method:

```java
    //Recursive DFS function to find all flights between source and destination
    private void dfs(String src, String dest, Set<String> visited,
```

```
                    Stack<String> path) {
    visited.add(src);

    if (src.equals(dest)) {
      printPath(path);
    } else {
      for (String flight : cities.get(src).flights.keySet()) {
        if (!visited.contains(flight)) {
          path.push(flight);
          dfs(flight, dest, visited, path);
          path.pop();
        }
      }
    }

    visited.remove(src);
  }
```

Listing 14-6: Flights.java

The dfs() method in the FlightGraph class implements *Depth-First Search (DFS)* recursively to find all possible flights between a source and a destination city within a flight network.

It begins by marking the current city as visited and checks if it matches the destination city. If the destination is reached, it prints the current path. Otherwise, it explores all neighboring cities not yet visited by recursively calling itself for each neighbor.

During exploration, it pushes the neighboring city onto the path stack and continues the search until all possible paths from the current city are explored or until the destination is reached.

Upon backtracking, it removes the current city from the path stack and marks it as unvisited, allowing exploration of alternative paths. This process is repeated until all cities in the network are explored.

We use the aforementioned stack to print the final path in PrintPath() method:

```
  //Helper function to print a path (stack content)
  private void printPath(Stack<String> path) {
    System.out.println(String.join(" -> ", path));
  }
}
```

Listing 14-7: Flights.java

Finally in main(), we add cities and flights to the graph and we ask the user to select a pair of cities to calculate the best (cheapest) combination of flights:

```
public static void main(String[] args) {
  Scanner scanner = new Scanner(System.in);
  FlightGraph graph = new FlightGraph();
```

```java
        graph.addCity("London");
        graph.addCity("Paris");
        graph.addCity("Berlin");
        graph.addCity("Rome");
        graph.addCity("Madrid");
        graph.addCity("Amsterdam");

        graph.addFlight("London", "Paris", 100);
        graph.addFlight("London", "Berlin", 150);
        graph.addFlight("London", "Madrid", 200);
        graph.addFlight("Paris", "Berlin", 120);
        graph.addFlight("Paris", "Rome", 180);
        graph.addFlight("Berlin", "Rome", 220);
        graph.addFlight("Madrid", "Rome", 250);
        graph.addFlight("Madrid", "Amsterdam", 170);
        graph.addFlight("Amsterdam", "Berlin", 130);

        System.out.print("Enter departure city: ");
        String departure = scanner.nextLine();
        System.out.print("Enter destination city: ");
        String destination = scanner.nextLine();

        //Display all possible flights
        System.out.println("All possible flights between " + departure
            + " and " + destination + ":");
        graph.displayAllFlights(departure, destination);

        //Find the cheapest route and total price
        Map<String, Integer> dist = new HashMap<>();
        List<String> route = graph.findCheapestRoute(departure, destination, dist);
        int totalPrice = dist.get(destination);

        //Display the cheapest route and total price
        System.out.print("Cheapest Route: ");
        System.out.println(String.join(" -> ", route));
        System.out.println("Total Price: " + totalPrice);
    }
}
```

Listing 14-8: Flights.java

You can find this project in GitHub:

https://github.com/htset/java_exercises_dsa/tree/master/Flights

15. MNIST Image Comparison

In this exercise, we will play with handwriting images from the MNIST database.

Proposed Solution

The MNIST database (http://yann.lecun.com/exdb/mnist/) is a set of images depicting handwritten digits. The images are of 28x28 dimension and are typically used when studying pattern recognition and machine learning techniques.

Source: Wikipedia

We will download the following file and we will unzip it in our project's directory:

http://yann.lecun.com/exdb/mnist/train-images-idx3-ubyte.gz

We will also rename it as *input.dat*.

The first 15 bytes of this file, contain metadata about the images, i.e. the number of the images and their dimensions. Therefore, we will start reading from the 16th byte in steps of 28x28=784 bytes.

First, we define the `Image` class that will store the image data in an array of `byte`:

```
package MNISTImages;

import java.io.*;
import java.util.ArrayList;
import java.util.List;
```

```java
import java.util.Random;

class Image {
  public byte[] data;
  public int id;

  public Image(byte[] data, int id) {
    this.data = new byte[data.length];
    System.arraycopy(data, 0, this.data, 0, data.length);
    this.id = id;
  }

  public void print() {
    for (int i = 0; i < data.length; i++) {
      if (data[i] == 0)
        System.out.print(" ");
      else
        System.out.print("*");
      if ((i + 1) % 28 == 0)
        System.out.println();
    }
  }

  public double euclideanDistance(Image img) {
    double distance = 0.0;
    for (int i = 0; i < data.length; i++) {
      distance += Math.sqrt(Math.pow((data[i] - img.data[i]), 2));
    }
    return Math.sqrt(distance);
  }
}
```

Listing 15-1: MNISTImages.java

Inside the class, we implement the `Image` constructor and a method that prints the image as a series of asterisks.

We also implement the method that will calculate the *Euclidean distance* between two images, the current image and another one passed as method parameter. We are essentially calculating the sum of the differences between the respective bytes of two images. If the images are similar in content, then the distance will be minimized. Conversely, the distance will be higher, for images that have significant differences.

Now, let's see the `main()` method:

```java
public class MNISTImages {
  static final int ImageSize = 784;
  static final int MetaDataSize = 15;

  public static void main(String[] args) {
    List<Image> images = new ArrayList<>();

    try (FileInputStream ifs = new FileInputStream("input.dat")) {
```

```
      //Skip the metadata at the beginning of the file
      ifs.skip(MetaDataSize);

      byte[] pixels = new byte[ImageSize];
      int count = 0;
      //Read data from the file and insert images into the list
      while (ifs.read(pixels) > 0) {
        images.add(new Image(pixels, count++));
      }
    } catch (IOException e) {
      e.printStackTrace();
    }

    System.out.println("Total images: " + (images.size() - 1));

    //Example: Find the closest image to a randomly selected image
    //Seed the random number generator
    Random rand = new Random();

    //Generate a random index within the range of the list length
    int randomIndex = rand.nextInt(images.size());
    System.out.println("Random index: " + randomIndex);

    Image randomImage = images.get(randomIndex);
    randomImage.print();

    Image closestImage = null;
    double minDistance = Double.POSITIVE_INFINITY;
    int minIndex = 0;

    for (int i = 0; i < images.size(); i++) {
      double distance = randomImage.euclideanDistance(images.get(i));
      if (distance != 0 && distance < minDistance) {
        minDistance = distance;
        minIndex = i;
        closestImage = images.get(i);
      }
    }

    //Output the label of the closest image
    System.out.println("\nClosest image (distance=" + minDistance +
        ", index = " + minIndex + ")\n");

    //Print closest image
    closestImage.print();
  }
}
```

Listing 15-2: MNISTImages.java

We use an `ArrayList` object to store the image references. After we open the *input.dat* binary file, we skip the first 15 bytes with `skip()`. Then, in a loop, we read one image at a time (784 bytes) with `read()` into a buffer and we copy them to the respective `Image` object into the list.

Afterwards, we get a randomly selected image from the list, and we print it using empty space where the byte is zero and an asterisk ('*') in places where the image bytes are non-zero. This way, we can get an idea of the handwriting digit that was chosen:

After printing the selected image, we iterate the images list, and we calculate the Euclidian distance between the randomly selected image and the currently selected image from the list. We maintain the minimum distance encountered and the corresponding image along with its ID.

At the end, we print the closest image that we got; it seems that the algorithm is working fine.

As a final note, this algorithm will take a lot of time to get the closest image, as it is checking all the images, one by one. There are other algorithms that will make this operation faster, albeit, with a loss of precision.

One such example is the Locality-Sensitive Hashing[2] (LSH) algorithm, a technique used for approximate nearest neighbor search in high-dimensional spaces. LSH is particularly useful when dealing with large datasets where traditional exact nearest neighbor search methods become computationally expensive.

You can find this project in GitHub:

https://github.com/htset/java_exercises_dsa/tree/master/MNISTImages

---

[2] https://en.wikipedia.org/wiki/Locality-sensitive_hashing

16. HTTP Server with Caching

In this exercise, we will create a simple HTTP server that will serve static content (only HTML files). The web server will make use of a cache mechanism that will keep the most recently served content, in order to boost the server's performance.

Proposed Solution

The web server cache is a structure that stores the content that was previously sent to the client browser. The cache has limited space, so when it is filled up, we will need to empty the *least recently used (LRU)* entry in order to make space for the new entry. Moreover, when an entry is used by the server to send content to the client, then this entry is moved to the head of the list, as it is the more recently used entry.

Let's see the cache definition:

```
package WebServerCache;

public class LRUCache {
  static final int CACHE_SIZE = 3;
  Node head;
  Node tail;
  int size;

  static class Node {
    String url;
    String content;
    Node prev;
    Node next;
  }

  public LRUCache() {
    size = 0;
    head = null;
    tail = null;
  }

  ...
```

Listing 16-1: LRUCache.java

The cache is implemented as a *doubly linked list*. In this kind of linked list, we can move to both directions, forward and backward. The doubly linked list is beneficial in our case as we can efficiently remove and insert nodes anywhere in the list without needing to traverse the list from the beginning. The same effect could be achieved with simple linked lists, or even arrays, but with lower performance.

Let's skip the rest of the cache definition for now, and jump to the `main()` method of our program:

```java
  public static void main(String[] args) {
    HttpServer server = new HttpServer();
    try {
      server.start();
    } catch (IOException e) {
      e.printStackTrace();
    }
  }
}
```

Listing 16-2: WebServerCache.java

Here, we create an object of the HttpServer class, that will handle the connections with the clients. Let's see how it is implemented:

```java
package WebServerCache;

import java.io.*;
import java.net.*;
import java.nio.charset.StandardCharsets;
import java.nio.file.Files;

class HttpServer {
  static final int PORT = 8080;
  static final int MAX_REQUEST_SIZE = 1024;
  LRUCache cache;

  public HttpServer() {
    cache = new LRUCache();
  }

  public void start() throws IOException {
    //Open server socket
    ServerSocket server = new ServerSocket(PORT);
    System.out.println("Server started on port " + PORT);

    while (true) {
      //Wait for connections
      Socket client = server.accept();
      handleRequest(client);
      client.close();
    }
  }

  void handleRequest(Socket client) throws IOException {
    //Read request
    InputStream inputStream = client.getInputStream();
    byte[] buffer = new byte[MAX_REQUEST_SIZE];
    int bytesRead = inputStream.read(buffer);
    String request = new String(buffer, 0, bytesRead, StandardCharsets.UTF_8);
    System.out.println("Received request: " + request);

    //Find request type (GET)
    String[] parts = request.split(" ");
    if (parts.length < 2 || !parts[0].equals("GET")) {
```

```java
      System.out.println("Invalid request format.");
      return;
    }

    //Get request url and check whether it is already stored in the cache
    String url = parts[1];
    String content = cache.getContent(url);

    if (content.isEmpty()) {
      //If not found in cache, read it from the HTML file
      try {
        content = new String(Files.readAllBytes(new File(url.substring(1)).toPath()),
                        StandardCharsets.UTF_8);
        System.out.println("Got content from file: " + content);
        cache.putContent(url, content);
      } catch (FileNotFoundException e) {
        System.out.println("File not found: " + url.substring(1));
        content = "HTTP/1.1 404 Not Found\r\n\r\n";
      } catch (IOException e) {
        System.out.println("File not found: " + url.substring(1));
        content = "HTTP/1.1 404 Not Found\r\n\r\n";
      }

    } else {
      System.out.println("Serving content from cache.");
    }

    //Check if the content is HTML or plain text
    String contentType = "text/plain"; //Default content type is plain text
    if (url.endsWith(".html") || url.endsWith(".htm")) {
      //If the URL ends with .html or .htm, it's HTML content
      contentType = "text/html";
    }

    //Build the response
    String response = "HTTP/1.1 200 OK\r\nContent-Type: "
        + contentType + "\r\n\r\n" + content;

    byte[] responseBytes = response.getBytes(StandardCharsets.UTF_8);
    OutputStream outputStream = client.getOutputStream();
    outputStream.write(responseBytes);
  }
```

Listing 16-3: WebServerCache.java

Here we create a `ServerSocket` object that continuously accepts HTTP connections from web browsers at port 8080. When a connection is accepted, then the `handleRequest()` method is called.

Initially, the web request stream is received into the `buffer` byte array. Then we create a string object that will contain the request. The string is split in order to retrieve the request type and the URL; only GET requests are handled by our server.

We then use the request URL to search in the cache for a previously stored response for this URL. If such an entry is not found in the cache, then we open the requested HTML file (The HTML files are stored in the same folder as our executable), and we transmit its HTML content in the response. Note that, before sending the content, we must send the header of the response:

```
HTTP/1.1 200 OK\nContent-Type: text/html
```

If the URL is found in the cache, then we get the content from there and we send it with the response.

Let's see how we do this, in method getContent() from the LRUCache class:

```java
//Get the content associated with a URL from the cache
public String getContent(String url) {
  Node current = head;
  while (current != null) {
    if (current.url.equals(url)) {
      moveToHead(current);
      System.out.println("Got content from cache: " + current.content);
      return current.content;
    }
    current = current.next;
  }
  return "";
}
```

Listing 16-4: LRUCache.java

We start from the head of the list, and we search for the URL in the cache's nodes. If we find the URL, then we move the node to the head of the cache (the *most recently used entry*) and we return the stored HTML content. The method returns an empty string if the URL is not found in the cache.

When a page is read from its file, then we store its content into the cache, with putContent():

```java
//Put a URL-content pair into the cache
public void putContent(String url, String content) {
  if (size == CACHE_SIZE) {
    deleteNode(tail);
    size--;
  }
  Node newNode = createNode(url, content);
  insertAtHead(newNode);
  size++;
}
```

Listing 16-5: LRUCache.java

If we have reached the maximum cache size, then the *LRU algorithm* kicks in: we delete the least recently used entry (the node at the tail of the list) and we make space for the insertion of the new entry (at the head of the list).

Now we can examine the methods that handle the cache operations. First, let's see how we can create a new node:

```java
//Create a new node
Node createNode(String url, String content) {
  Node newNode = new Node();
  newNode.url = url;
  newNode.content = content;
  newNode.prev = null;
  newNode.next = null;
  System.out.println("New node created: " + content);
  return newNode;
}
```
Listing 16-6: LRUCache.java

Next, we see how to insert a new node at the head of the cache:

```java
//Insert a new node at the head of the cache
void insertAtHead(Node node) {
  node.next = head;
  node.prev = null;
  if (head != null)
    head.prev = node;
  head = node;
  if (tail == null)
    tail = node;
  System.out.println("Node inserted at head: " + node.content);
}
```
Listing 16-7: LRUCache.java

Note that in all operations we have to take care of all four references: head, tail, next, prev.

As part of the LRU algorithm, we have to move a node to the head of the list:

```java
//Move a node to the head of the cache
void moveToHead(Node node) {
  if (node == head)
    return;
  if (node.prev != null)
    node.prev.next = node.next;
  if (node.next != null)
    node.next.prev = node.prev;
  node.prev = null;
  node.next = head;
  if (head != null)
    head.prev = node;
```

```
    head = node;
    if (tail == null)
      tail = node;
    System.out.println("Node moved to head: " + node.content);
  }
```
Listing 16-8: LRUCache.java

Finally, here is the code for node deletion:

```
//Delete a node from the cache
void deleteNode(Node node) {
  if (node == null)
    return;
  if (node == head)
    head = node.next;
  if (node == tail)
    tail = node.prev;
  if (node.prev != null)
    node.prev.next = node.next;
  if (node.next != null)
    node.next.prev = node.prev;
  System.out.println("Node deleted: " + node.content);
  }
}
```
Listing 16-9: LRUCache.java

You can find this project in GitHub:

https://github.com/htset/java_exercises_dsa/tree/master/WebServerCache

17. Distributed Auction

In this exercise, we will create a distributed auction, that will consist of an auction server that receives bids from multiple clients. The clients will communicate with the server via sockets. The server will wait for 20 seconds (using a timer) for a new bid, or else the auction is over and the maximum bid wins. The timer will be reset upon timely submission of new bid.

Proposed Solution

Let's start wih the auction server. The server should be able to accommodate multiple clients. For this reason, each client will be served in a separate *thread*, that will be spawned when the server socket accepts a new connection:

```java
package AuctionServer;

import java.io.*;
import java.net.*;
import java.nio.charset.StandardCharsets;
import java.util.Timer;
import java.util.TimerTask;

public class AuctionServer {

  //Client class representing each client connected to the server
  static class Client {
    private final Socket socket;
    private final BufferedWriter writer;
    private final int id;

    //Constructor for the Client class
    public Client(Socket socket, int id) throws IOException {
      this.socket = socket;
      //Setting up writer to send data to the client
      this.writer
        = new BufferedWriter(
            new OutputStreamWriter(socket.getOutputStream(),
                                   StandardCharsets.UTF_8));
      this.id = id;
    }

    public Socket getSocket() {
      return socket;
    }

    public BufferedWriter getWriter() {
      return writer;
    }

    public int getId() {
      return id;
    }
```

}
...

Listing 17-1: AuctionServer.java

Here we define the Client class as a static class inside the AuctionServer class. Client stores information about the connected client (its ID and the corresponding Socket and BufferedWriter objects).

Next, we have the definition of some constants and the class properties:

```java
//Constants
private static final int PORT = 8080; //Port number for the server
private static final int MAX_CLIENTS = 5; //Maximum number of clients

//Server and clients
private static ServerSocket server;
private static Client[] clients = new Client[MAX_CLIENTS]; //Array to hold clients

//Auction details
private static int bestBid = 0; //Highest bid received
private static int winningClient = 0; //Client ID of the highest bidder

//Timer for auction end
private static Timer timer;
```

Listing 17-2: AuctionServer.java

Now we present the main() method:

```java
public static void main(String[] args) {
  try {
    server = new ServerSocket(PORT); //Setting up the server socket
    System.out.println("Server listening on port " + PORT);

    //Start the timer
    timer = new Timer();
    timer.schedule(new TimerTask() {
      @Override
      public void run() {
        timerCompletionRoutine();
      }
    }, 20000, 20000); //Schedule the timer to trigger every 20 seconds

    while (true) {
      //Accept a new client connection
      Socket clientSocket = server.accept();
      System.out.println("Client connected: "
          + clientSocket.getRemoteSocketAddress());

      //Find an available slot for the client
      int clientId = -1;
      for (int i = 0; i < MAX_CLIENTS; i++) {
```

```
          if (clients[i] == null) {
            clientId = i;
            clients[i] = new Client(clientSocket, clientId + 1);
            System.out.println("Client no. " + (clientId + 1) + " connected.");
            break;
          }
        }

        //Handle client in a separate thread
        int finalClientId = clientId;
        new Thread(() -> handleClient(finalClientId)).start();
      }
    } catch (Exception ex) {
      System.out.println("Server error: " + ex.getMessage());
    } finally {
      try {
        if (server != null) server.close();
      } catch (IOException e) {
        e.printStackTrace();
      }
    }
  }
}
```

Listing 17-3: AuctionServer.java

We open a new `ServerSocket` and we listen for new connections.

We also start a timer with 20 seconds duration. When the timer expires, then the `timerCompletionRoutine()` method will be called, ending the auction process.

When a new connection arrives, we store the client details in the clients' array and we spawn a new thread. The thread will run the `handleClient()` method, that will handle the communication with the specific client.

Now, let's see the `handleClient()` method:

```
//Handle client bids
private static void handleClient(int clientId) {
  try {
    Client client = clients[clientId];
    Socket clientSocket = client.getSocket();
    BufferedReader reader
        = new BufferedReader(
            new InputStreamReader(clientSocket.getInputStream(),
              StandardCharsets.UTF_8));

    String bid;
    while (true) {
      //Read a bid from the client
      bid = reader.readLine();
      if (bid == null) {
        //Client disconnected
        System.out.println("Client disconnected: "
            + clientSocket.getRemoteSocketAddress());
```

```
          clients[clientId] = null;
          break;
        }

        int bidAmount = Integer.parseInt(bid);
        System.out.println("Received bid " + bidAmount + " from client "
            + client.getId());

        synchronized (AuctionServer.class) {
          if (bidAmount > bestBid) {
            bestBid = bidAmount;
            winningClient = client.getId();

            String msg = "New best bid: " + bestBid
                + " (Client: " + winningClient + ")";
            broadcastMessage(msg);
            System.out.println("New best bid: " + bestBid
                + " (Client: " + winningClient + ")");

            //Reset the timer
            timer.cancel();
            timer = new Timer();
            timer.schedule(new TimerTask() {
              @Override
              public void run() {
                timerCompletionRoutine();
              }
            }, 20000, 20000);
          } else {
            String msg = "Received lower bid. Best bid remains at: " + bestBid;
            broadcastMessage(msg);
            System.out.println("Received lower bid. Best bid remains at: "
                + bestBid);
          }
        }
      }
    } catch (Exception ex) {
      System.out.println("Client error: " + ex.getMessage());
    }
  }
}
```

Listing 17-4: AuctionServer.java

This method takes care of the communication with the client. It gets as input the client's ID, that was passed in `main()`:

`new Thread(() -> handleClient(finalClientId)).start();`

Then, in an endless `while` loop, it blocks in the `reader.readLine()` method, waiting for input from the client. When a message arrives, the method is unblocked and continues to check the input. If the bid is null, then the client has disconnected.

If the client has actually sent a valid bid, we compare it with the current maximum bid and we update this value if we got a higher bid. We also proceed with informing all clients about the submitted bid. We also reset the timer to get a new 20 seconds' period.

Here, bestBid and winningClient are shared resources that might be accessed and modified by multiple client handler threads. To protect these shared resources, we synchronize the critical sections where these variables are read or written.

Next, we define the broadcastMessage() method, that sends messages to the clients:

```java
//Broadcast message to all clients
private static void broadcastMessage(String msg) throws IOException {
  for (int i = 0; i < MAX_CLIENTS; i++) {
    if (clients[i] != null) {
      clients[i].getWriter().write(msg);
      clients[i].getWriter().newLine();
      clients[i].getWriter().flush();
    }
  }
}
```

Listing 17-5: AuctionServer.java

When the timer eventually expires, the timerCompletionRoutine() method will be called:

```java
//Timer completion routine when auction ends
private static void timerCompletionRoutine() {
  System.out.println("Auction finished. Winning bid: " + bestBid
      + ", winner: client no. " + winningClient);

  String msg = "Auction finished. Winning bid: " + bestBid
      + ", winner: client no. " + winningClient;
  try {
    broadcastMessage(msg);
  } catch (IOException e) {
    e.printStackTrace();
  }

  //Exit the program
  System.exit(0);
  }
}
```

Listing 17-6: AuctionServer.java

After informing all clients about the winning bid, we exit the program. The client sockets will be closed by the respective clients when they receive the message of the auction completion.

Now for the auction client, we first implement the main() method:

```java
package AuctionClient;

import java.io.*;
import java.net.*;
import java.nio.charset.StandardCharsets;

public class AuctionClient {

    private static final int PORT = 8080; //Port number to connect to the server
    private static final String SERVER_IP = "127.0.0.1"; //Server IP address

    private static Socket client;
    private static boolean isRunning = true;
    private static Thread receiveThread;

    public static void main(String[] args) {
        //Connect to the server
        try {
            client = new Socket(SERVER_IP, PORT);
            System.out.println("Connected to server.");
        } catch (Exception ex) {
            System.out.println("Connect failed: " + ex.getMessage());
            return;
        }

        //Start receive handler thread
        receiveThread = new Thread(AuctionClient::receiveHandler);
        receiveThread.start();

        //Send bids until the user quits
        try (BufferedReader consoleReader
                    = new BufferedReader(new InputStreamReader(System.in));
             BufferedWriter writer
                    = new BufferedWriter(new OutputStreamWriter(client.getOutputStream(),
                    StandardCharsets.UTF_8))) {

            String bid;
            while (isRunning) {
                System.out.print("\nEnter your bid (or 'q' to quit): ");
                bid = consoleReader.readLine();

                if ("q".equalsIgnoreCase(bid)) {
                    isRunning = false;
                    client.close();
                    receiveThread.interrupt(); //Interrupt the receive thread
                    break;
                }

                try {
                    writer.write(bid);
                    writer.newLine();
                    writer.flush();
                } catch (Exception ex) {
                    System.out.println("Send failed: " + ex.getMessage());
```

```
          return;
        }
      }
    } catch (IOException e) {
      e.printStackTrace();
    }

    //Ensure client is closed
    try {
      client.close();
    } catch (IOException e) {
      e.printStackTrace();
    }
  }
```

Listing 17-7: AuctionClient.java

Here, we create a `Socket` object, and we connect to the server. If the connection is successful, we spawn a new thread that will be used to receive and print the information from the server.

The sending part of the communication, i.e. the submission of bids to the server, will be performed by the main thread. If we had the same thread handle sending and receiving of data, we would have a problem, as the `readLine()` method would block and would not let the user send a new bid.

Here is the callback method for the thread handler:

```
//Handle incoming messages from the server
private static void receiveHandler() {
  try (BufferedReader reader
      = new BufferedReader(
          new InputStreamReader(client.getInputStream(), StandardCharsets.UTF_8))) {
    while (isRunning) {
      try {
        if (Thread.interrupted()) {
          break; //Exit if the thread is interrupted
        }
        String message = reader.readLine();
        if (message == null || message.isEmpty()) {
          System.out.println("\nServer disconnected.");
          break;
        }

        System.out.println("\nServer: " + message);

        if (message.startsWith("Auction")) {
          System.out.println("Auction ended. Exiting program.");
          isRunning = false;
          break;
        }
      } catch (IOException ex) {
        if (isRunning) {
```

```
            //Check if still running to avoid printing
            // error when stopping intentionally
            System.out.println("Receive failed: " + ex.getMessage());
          }
          break;
        }
      }
    } catch (IOException e) {
      if (isRunning) {
        //Check if still running to avoid printing
        // error when stopping intentionally
        e.printStackTrace();
      }
    }
  }
}
```

Listing 17-6: AuctionClient.java

This thread receives messages from the auction server and prints them in the console. When the final message, starting with "Auction" arrives, then it closes down the resources and exits the program.

You can find this project in GitHub:

https://github.com/htset/java_exercises_dsa/tree/master/AuctionServer

https://github.com/htset/java_exercises_dsa/tree/master/AuctionClient